The School of Education

PETER LANG
New York • Washington, D.C./Baltimore • Boston
Bern • Frankfurt am Main • Berlin • Vienna • Paris

Jianping Shen

The School of Education

Its Mission, Faculty, and Reward Structure

PETER LANG
New York • Washington, D.C./Baltimore • Boston
Bern • Frankfurt am Main • Berlin • Vienna • Paris

Library of Congress Cataloging-in-Publication Data

Shen, Jianping.
The school of education: its mission, faculty,
and reward structure / Jianping Shen.
p. cm.
Includes bibliographical references and index.
1. Teachers colleges—United States. 2. Teacher educators—
United States. I. Title.
LB2165.S54   370'.71'0973—dc21   98-25596
ISBN 0-8204-4090-6

Die Deutsche Bibliothek-CIP-Einheitsaufnahme

Shen, Jianping:
The school of education: its mission, faculty,
and reward structure / Jianping Shen. –New York; Washington, D.C./Baltimore;
Boston; Bern; Frankfurt am Main; Berlin; Vienna; Paris: Lang.
ISBN 0-8204-4090-6

Cover design by Lisa Dillon

The paper in this book meets the guidelines for permanence and durability
of the Committee on Production Guidelines for Book Longevity
of the Council of Library Resources.

© 1999 Peter Lang Publishing, Inc., New York

Printed in the United States of America

CONTENTS

CHAPTER ONE

The School of Education and Its Faculty: An Overview

Faculty members in the school of education have a multi-dimensional mission. The traditional conceptualization of this mission—teaching, research, and service—is embodied in different ways for individual faculty members in various types of higher education institutions. The education faculty members' mission is reinforced by the reward structure, which, as many studies suggest, places paramount importance on research. Therefore, there is a discrepancy between the ideal expectation for the education faculty members' multi-dimensional mission and the uni-dimensional reward structure. In essence, there is an internal tension between what is expected and what is rewarded within the context of the school of education. The school of education does not exist in a vacuum; society as a whole holds some expectations for the school of education, the most important of which is the education of school educators. Therefore, from the perspective of society, there is an external tension between the current status of, and the public's expectation for, the school of education. The purpose of this book is to examine the mission, faculty, and reward structure in the school of education. It seeks to depict the current status of the school of education and provide some empirical data for discussing its future.

This introductory chapter, which provides a context for the book, is divided into four interrelated parts. It begins with a brief history of the evolution of the institutional context for the school of education. In connection with this context, it proceeds to discuss the enlargement of the mission for education faculty members. This introductory chapter then inquires into the composition of education faculty members and the uneasy relationship among the subgroups. Finally, the discussion extrapolates the tension within the school of education to the societal context in order to discuss the function and well-being of the school of education. The logic of this chapter is developed as follows: with the understanding that the mission for education faculty members becomes more and more encompassing, and that subgroups of education faculty members have developed in association with various missions of the school of education, how the promotion criteria equitably reward education faculty members should be under scrutiny. What complicates the situation in the school of education is the changing context of the higher education institution of which the school is a part. With the evolution of the higher education institution, research is more and more emphasized and the origin of the school of education is gradually forgotten. Thus the question of what the school of education is all about emerges.

Evolution of the Institutional Context of the School of Education

The institutional context of the school of education has been changing over the years. This is certainly true of the schools of education situated in those institutions that evolved from normal schools to teachers' colleges to state colleges and then to regional state universities, as described by Goodlad (1990a, 1990b) and Smith (1990). The changing institutional context also rings true for those schools of education situated in elite research universities, as studied by Clifford and Guthrie (1988), although most of the schools studied by Clifford and Guthrie are in research-oriented private universities and do not follow the evolutionary path described above. Clifford and Guthrie's inquiry into the beacon schools of education and Goodlad and his associates' study of a representative sample of 29 schools have quite different samples, but their studies reveal some parallel patterns in the evolution of the institutional context.

The evolutionary process from normal schools to regional state universities is the very evidence of the changing institutional context for the school of education. The preparation of teachers used to be the sole or major mission of many higher education institutions, but it now is only one of the missions in the "multiversity" (Soder & Sirotnik, 1990). Especially in the last 25 years, there has been a profound shift in the balance of the various missions of the school of education. Scholarly work has risen to preeminence at the expense of teaching and service (Goodlad, 1990b, pp. 154–195).

Concurrent with the rising importance of research, schools of education tend to retreat from the model of professional education and incline toward the model of academic education that prevails in the arts and sciences. The inclination toward the model of academic education is not only reflected in the moving away from teaching and service to more engagement in research, but is also revealed in moving away from the preparation of teachers and to engagement in the preparation of more specialized personnel at the graduate level. In many cases, the more a school of education distances itself from the preparation of teachers, the more respect the school commands in the academic community. Most of the five top-ranked schools in Cartter's (1977) rating of leading schools of education had little or no involvement in teacher education. This is perhaps true with individual faculty members as well. Faculty members with high status distance themselves from the preparation of teachers or avoid teaching altogether.

Nonetheless, "the professionalization of education through the route of academic specialization in university-oriented schools of education was both fragmenting the field and loosening the bonds between professional practice and professional education" (Clifford & Guthrie, 1988, p. 117). The tension between the academic model and the professional model is one of the themes in the evolution of schools of education (Clifford & Guthrie, 1988; Soder & Sirotnik, 1990).

The inclination of the school of education to the academic education model is partly related to the low status of teacher education on campus in the changing institutional context. Teaching, as a primarily feminine occupation, is low in status (Clifford & Guthrie, 1988; Goodlad, 1990b). Accordingly, teacher education, in particular, and the school of education and its faculty, in general, have relatively low status on the university campus (Goodlad, 1990b; Lasley, 1986; McConnell, Anderson, & Hunter, 1962). Ducharme and Agne (1986) described education faculty members as being among "the least welcome guests at the educational lawn party of the establishment of higher education." With the rising emphasis on research in higher education institutions in the last quarter-century (Boyer, 1990), the low status of education faculty members has been exacerbated. Under these institutional pressures, schools of education choose to emulate the norms of the arts and sciences rather than those of professional schools, such as medical and law. Nonetheless, education faculty members are generally still looked down upon as second-class citizens on campuses for their perceived mediocre scholarship (Clark, 1987; Ducharme & Agne, 1986; Schwebel, 1985, 1989).

In summary, the evolution of the institutional context gradually moves the school of education away from its once central mission of the preparation of teachers to more research-oriented activities, and the school of education tends to emulate the arts and sciences rather than professional schools such as law and medical schools. However, albeit the efforts made by the education faculty to emulate those in the arts and sciences, education faculty members do not enjoy the same status as their colleagues in the arts and sciences. All these give rise to a serious question regarding the mission of the school of education and its faculty in the context of the ever changing institutional environment. With the evolution of the institutional context, the missions for the school of education and its faculty become diversified and, to a certain degree, fragmented. The next section will continue to inquire into how the missions of the school of education become enlarged and fragmented.

A Brief History of the Development of the Faculty's Mission

It is generally held that William Harold Payne, Chair in the Science and the Art of Teaching, hired by the University of Michigan in 1879, was the first professor of education (e.g., Culbertson, 1988; Hazlett, 1989; Howey & Zimpher, 1990; Johanningmeier & Johnson, 1975). Thus the education professoriate in the United States has a history of about 120 years. During this time, the society and the institutions in which education professors work have undergone dramatic changes. The mission of the emergent education professoriate was almost exclusively the preparation of school teachers, particularly secondary school teachers since elementary school teachers were educated in normal schools before they evolved into state colleges and universities. The observation that the preparation of school teachers was the major responsibility of the early education professoriate is implied in Payne's official title—Chair in the Science and the Art of Teaching.

Powell's (1980) inquiry into the education professoriate at Harvard and Allison's (1989) case study of three early professors at the University of Tennessee also attest to the importance of the preparation of school teachers for the emergent education professoriate. For example, in the late nineteenth century, Eliot, then the president of Harvard University, was concerned about the quality of freshmen. He and Harvard's faculty believed that better prepared teachers would result in better prepared students (Powell, 1980). Paul Henry Hanus, a professor of mathematics and a high school principal in Denver, was then hired to coordinate Harvard's teacher education program during the 1890–1891 academic year. He was brought to Harvard "not for his scholarly potential but as an administrative convenience, as someone to take charge of the details of teacher education" (Hazlett, 1989, p. 20).

The mission of the preparation of school teachers was followed by the mission of the preparation of school administrators in the beginning of the twentieth century. Interestingly, Payne was extolled as one of the pioneers in preparing school administrators (Culbertson, 1988), and Hanus moved from a teacher educator to a specialist in school administration during his twenty-year tenure at Harvard. By 1910, he considered himself an expert in school administration (Hazlett, 1989), presumably an expertise of more significance than that in teacher education.

The education of school teachers and administrators has been further supplemented by the preparation of other educators, such as special educators, school counselors, and school psychologists. Following the development of counselor education after the National Defense Act, preparation of special educators has gained momentum since 1975, the year of the enactment of the Education for All Handicapped Children Act (PL 94-142) (Wang, Reynolds, & Walberg, 1987, p. ix). The foregoing supports Katz's (1966) observation that the programs, courses, and professoriate in education have developed according to the role of personnel in the lower school system.

According to Boyer (1990), American higher education first devoted itself primarily to the intellectual and moral development of students, then added service as a mission. The third dimension of the faculty members' responsibilities, advancement of knowledge through research, had taken firm root in American higher education by the late nineteenth century, and has matured since World War II. Boyer (1990, p. 11) describes the culmination of research in the following paragraph:

> In 1958, Theodore Caplow and Reece McGee defined this new reality when they observed that while young faculty were hired as *teachers*, they were evaluated primarily as *researchers*. This shift in expectations is vividly revealed in two national surveys conducted by The Carnegie Foundation for the Advancement of Teaching. Twenty-one percent of the faculty surveyed in 1969 strongly agreed that it is difficult to achieve tenure without publishing. By 1989, the number had doubled, to 42 percent. The change at comprehensive colleges— from 6 percent to 43 percent—is especially noteworthy since these institutions have virtually no doctoral programs and only limited resources for research. Even at liberal arts colleges, where teaching has always been highly prized, nearly one in four faculty strongly agreed in 1989 that it is difficult to get tenure without publishing.

Historically, the central function of the emergent education professoriate was the education of teachers and other practitioners. The professoriate of education did not emerge out of the need for inquiry (Borrowman, 1975). Today, however, the connotation of "the ideal professor of education" includes conducting research, no matter what type of institution (Boyer, 1987; Wisniewski, 1989; Wisniewski & Ducharme, 1989a, 1989b). In some elite research universities, education faculty members engaged in research early on. For doctorate granting universities, and particularly for comprehensive universities and liberal arts colleges, conducting research is a recent phenomenon.

In addition to preparing educators and conducting research, education faculty members are also expected to provide professional service (Schwebel, 1989; Wisniewski, 1989). Although service may mean different things for faculty members in various types of institutions, a common core of the service is to relate to schools beyond participating in programs dealing with the education of educators. Many studies show that about 80% of education faculty members have experience in elementary and secondary schools as teachers or administrators (AACTE, 1987, 1988, 1990, 1992; Ducharme & Agne, 1982; Ducharme & Kluender, 1990; Goodlad, 1990b; Soder, 1989a), but the ivory tower stereotype does exist. There are indeed many constraints for faculty members in the school of education in providing service. These constraints include the accommodation of education faculty members to the perceived norms of the faculty of the arts and sciences and the research-oriented reward structure (Dixon & Ishler, 1992; Lawson, 1990; Sirotnik, 1991; Soder, 1991; Stoddart, 1993; Winitzky, Stoddart, & O'Keefe, 1992). The current school-university partnership movement is, among others, a reaction to the unsatisfactory status of service provided to schools by education faculty members (Sirotnik & Goodlad, 1988).

Diversification of the Faculty in the School of Education

As is the case of American faculty in general (Boyer, 1990), education faculty members have been taking on more and more missions. With the diversification of missions for education faculty members, there tends to be different groups primarily responsible for certain missions of the school of education. Some faculty members tend to be more involved in the preparation of school teachers, others more in the preparation of school administrators or special educators. Although research and service are supposedly required for all faculty in the school of education, research shows there is a wide range of involvement for faculty both within and across different types of institutions (AACTE, 1988; Gideonse, 1989; Soder, 1989a, 1990b). Shen's (1995) analysis suggests that education faculty members who are heavily involved in the preparation of school teachers can be statistically distinguished from other faculty by their perceptions of current involvement in the missions of the school of education and their perception of current and desired tenure criteria.

Corresponding to the development of multiple fronts for the education faculty members' work, the faculty in the school of education became heterogeneous, consisting of several distinguishable groups. James Earl Russell, who had a twenty-seven-year tenure as Dean of Teachers College, Columbia University, commented in 1924 on the systematic difference between professors of academic and professional orientations in his institution (Hazlett, 1989). Powell and Sizer (1969) echoed Russell's observation 25 years later when they discussed the difference between field- and discipline-oriented professors.

The composition of the education professoriate and the division therein was one of the topics of the Society of Professors of Education's *The Professor of Education: An Assessment of Conditions* (Bagley, 1975). Jackson's thesis—"Divided we stand: Observations on the internal organization of the education professoriate"— conceptualized a tripartite composition of the education professoriate: disciplinists ("whose academic orientation derives from, feeds upon, and sometimes contributes to one or more of the disciplines within the social sciences"), generalists ("those professors whose professional expertise spans a broad range of educational matters, particularly, though not exclusively, those having to do with the *systematic* quality of schooling and its ongoing operation"), and pedagogists ("who are chiefly concerned with the transmission of, and improvement upon, pedagogical techniques and materials within conventionally delineated curricular areas"). Jackson observed that the *raison d'être* of each of the three groups seemed abundantly clear. Yet in practice, "these three groups form at best an uneasy alliance, often marked by tension, bickering, and petty jealousies. In extreme cases, the conflicts between them lead to what Russell described as 'bloodshed'" (Jackson, 1975, pp. 64–65, 67).

The characterization of different groups of education faculty members can also be found in more recent literature (e.g., Clifford & Guthrie, 1988; Ducharme, 1987; Finkelstein, 1982; Judge, 1982; Lawson, 1990; Roemer & Martinello, 1982). Ducharme (1987) characterizes education professors as beasts of burden, facilitators, or academicians. Lawson (1990) describes the change of the origin of education faculty members from practitioner-turned-professors to practitioner-scholars and to professional education scholars. He categorizes the aforementioned three groups as residual, dominant, and emergent, respectively. The professional scholars are an emergent and increasingly powerful group because of the prestige they are perceived to bring to the school of education and because their work orientations are congruent with those of the faculty in the arts and sciences.

Clifford and Guthrie (1988, p. 40) summarize rather well the diversification of the education professoriate and the tension therein:

> For all their numbers, education faculty are an intellectually-fragmented group, more divided into "sects" than their nineteenth-century medical counterparts. Their mutual differences in training separate them from professors in arts, letters, and science departments on their campuses. Some are former elementary or secondary school teachers or administrators, who have carried a particular orientation into the college and university world. Still others have had no such experience and are proud of that fact. "Educationists" embody training in every conceivable discipline and some "have no discipline at all—*only Education!*" according to their detractors. While some capitalize on their "roots," others have rejected their past association.

The aforementioned configurations of education faculty members are defined from the perspective of orientation, function, background, or the evolution of the origin of the education faculty. In reality, there is no one-to-one correspondence between an education faculty member's background, orientation, and function in the school of education. Therefore, it is difficult, if not impossible, to delineate education faculty members from one single perspective. However, the foregoing literature review supports the observation that education faculty members are diversified in many respects. Consequently, the conduct of their work and the nature of rewards for their work become a significant issue that is manifested in two aspects: first, the congruence or incongruence between mission involvement and promotion criteria; and second, involvement in which missions is more rewarded than others.

Extrapolating the Internal Tension to a Larger Context

The aforementioned discussions of the changing institutional context of the school of education, the enlargement of the missions of the school of education, and the diversification of the education faculty were developed from the perspective of the tension within the school of education. If we view the internal tension from the perspective of societal expectation, the issue becomes the purpose of the school of education. In other words, the crucial issues are whether the new missions of the school of education are appropriately incorporated, what the central mission is for the school of education, and whether the conduct of the school of education satisfies the public's expectations.

Except for half a dozen schools of education in elite research universities, when the schools came into existence, the central and sole mission was clear—the education of school teachers. With the inclusion of school administrators, school counselors, school psychologists, and special educators, this central mission evolved into the education of school educators, which, as much research indicates, is not as highly rewarded as research. Therefore, the enlargement of the missions of the school of education and the increasing importance of research result in a dilemma as to balancing various missions, on the one hand, and manifesting a clear identity of the school of education, on the other.

From the perspective of society, schools of education and their faculty members are expected, among other things, to educate school educators, conduct research, and provide service to lower schools. The society would expect schools of education to achieve in all these missions; but most importantly, the society expects them to excel in educating school educators, particularly school teachers. Other missions of the school of education, including research, should always serve the purpose of improving the education of educators and, ultimately, the education in lower schools. Dewey (1929) admonished more than half a century ago that educational practice should form the problems of educational inquiry, since its purpose is to improve educational practice. However, there is a wide sentiment that research has not only risen to preeminence but also failed to establish a constructive relationship with educational practice. In a sense, research is widely conducted and highly rewarded, but the main impetus for conducting research seems to be prestige and publicity rather than serving the central mission of the school of education.

Therefore, there is an external tension between the conduct of the school of education and the public's expectation. The tension is largely reflected in the discrepancy between the public's major interest in the school of education's role in educating teachers and improving education in lower schools and its increasing emphasis on research-related activities. This tension leads the public not only to criticize but also to punish the school of education by withdrawing support in various forms. An interesting example is the downsizing and elimination of some schools of education in the state of Oregon. This raises the issue of the institutional well-being of the school of education and, ultimately, the legitimacy of its existence in the future. In short, with the enlargement of the missions of the school of education from the education of school teachers to the current multi-dimensional one, schools of education have to balance various missions, pursue the common good, and maintain the public's support.

Summary

This introductory chapter illustrates both the internal tension existing in the school of education and the external tension between the public's expectations for, and the conduct of, the school of education. The evolution of the institutional context for the school of education, the expansion of the education faculty members' mission, and the development of the subdivision within the education faculty give rise to concerns regarding the education faculty members' mission involvement, the reward structure, and the relationship between mission involvement and the reward structure. In the next few chapters, we will inquire more into the history and current status of the school of education.

CHAPTER TWO

History of the School of Education: A Perspective from the Concept of Pedagogy

This chapter inquires into the evolution of the concept of pedagogy in the United States and sheds some light on the historical context of the school of education. The chapter begins with an introduction to briefly delineate the evolution of the concept of pedagogy, traces the traditions of pedagogy associated with normal schools and universities, inquires into the changing connotation of the concept of pedagogy over the years, and finally discusses the implications for the current situation.

Introduction

The last one and a half centuries witnessed the rise, fall, and gradual resurrection of the concept of pedagogy. Until the first decade of the twentieth century, pedagogy was a prevailing concept. Chairs of pedagogy were established in more than 45 universities by 1890, and such distinguished scholars as John Dewey held the title of Head Professor of Philosophy and Pedagogy at the University of Chicago at the turn of the century. Advanced degrees in pedagogy were offered by, for example, New York University and the University of Wisconsin (e.g., Hollis, 1898; Maynard, 1924).

There were also many scholarly publications that bore the word "pedagogy" in their titles, such as in the following:

A Treatise on Pedagogy for Young Teachers (Hewett, 1884)
The History of Pedagogy (Compayre, 1885/1899)
The Elements of Pedagogy (White, 1886)
History of Pedagogy (Hailman, 1874)
Experimental Pedagogy (Lay, 1907/1936)
Fundamentals of Pedagogy (Higgins, 1923)

Nonetheless, in the United States, the word pedagogy has gradually disappeared since the turn of the century, and education has been used in lieu of "pedagogy."

However, recent years witnessed a gradual resurrection of the concept of pedagogy. For example, Smith (1980) inquired into the blueprints of a school of pedagogy; Gage (1985) summarized the research on pedagogy in his book entitled *Hard Gains in the Soft Sciences: The Case of Pedagogy*; Shulman (1987) and his colleagues studied teachers' knowledge base with a particular focus on pedagogical knowledge and pedagogical content knowledge; and Goodlad (1990b, 1994a) proposed the establishment of centers of pedagogy on university campuses.

In light of the renewed interest in the concept of pedagogy, this chapter inquires into the following questions: How did the concept of pedagogy evolve in the last one and a half centuries? What were the changes in the connotation of the concept in its evolutionary process? And what does the evolution of the concept mean for the identity of the school of education?

Two Traditions of Pedagogy

The etymology of a word usually tells us something about its original meaning and many other meanings derived from it later. Unfortunately, the term "pedagogy" has a very humble origin, which was described by Henderson (1913, p. 621) as follows:

The word [pedagogy] is derived from the Greeks, among whom a pedagogue was the person, usually, if not always, a slave, who attended the young boy, going with him to and from school, carrying his materials for study, looking out for his wants and exercising authority over him. It is supposed that the pedagogues were often such slaves as would be useless for other tasks, and that they were not held in much respect even by the children who were placed in their charge. The name thus acquired in ancient times a connotation of lack of esteem, if not of contempt, which it is not entirely shaken off in modern usage.

In the 1881 edition of *The Dictionary of Education and Instruction*, "pedagogy" was defined as "the science and art of giving instruction to children, particularly in school, or as by a school-teacher" (Kiddle & Schem, 1881, p. 230). In the 1913 edition of *A Cyclopedia of Education*, pedagogy was defined "to mean the science and art of teaching" (Henderson, 1913, p. 621).

A search in the University of Washington libraries reveals that pedagogy is not an entry in encyclopedias and handbooks published after 1913, with the exception of the 1959 edition of the *Dictionary of Education*, in which the entry for pedagogy appears as follows:

> 1) the art, practice, or profession of teaching; 2) the systematized learning or instruction concerning principles and methods of teaching and of student control and guidance; largely replaced by the term *education*. (Good, 1959, p. 387)

If the former two definitions have the connotation to integrate the science and art of teaching, then the latter definition seems to differentiate these two aspects of pedagogy. The two aspects seem to represent two traditions of pedagogy—pedagogy as a skill or craft as associated with normal schools, and pedagogy as a university study. The following is a discussion of these two traditions.

Pedagogy in Normal Schools

The first public normal school was established in Lexington, Massachusetts, in 1839 (Wright, 1930, p. 368). Other normal schools followed in that state and in other New England states, and the trend gradually spread to the rest of the nation, though not reaching the South until quite late in the nineteenth or the early twentieth century.

The advent of normal schools was inseparable from the development of common schools, with the 1830s and 1840s known in educational history as the decades of the common school movement in the United States (Cremin, 1980; Spring, 1990). Common schooling increased the enrollment, which, in turn, required a rapid increase in the number of teachers to staff the schools. How to adequately staff common schools was an enormous challenge (Urban, 1990).

There were several reasons why Horace Mann and his contemporaries considered existing academies and colleges inadequate for staffing common schools. First, it was regarded that teachers in academies and colleges were too thoroughly committed to nontechnical education. Second, even if graduates of the existing academies and colleges entered teaching, they usually abandoned teaching quickly. The expectation for the normal school—then a new type of teacher preparation institution—determined the nature of the normal school as a single-purpose institution, one that would train teachers for the common school (Urban, 1990). The single purpose of training teachers for elementary schools meant that the curriculum of the normal school would be mainly technical although academic subjects were also offered due to the low academic level of many normal school students.

Pangburn (1932) summarized the situation in normal schools as it existed in 1890 and indicated that, at least up to that time, there had been no great change in the normal school curriculum since the institution's founding about 50 years earlier. Work in academic subjects at normal schools was largely in subjects that made up the curriculum of the elementary school. Work in the professional sequence

> consisted of thirteen weeks in the History of Education, twenty-seven weeks in the Science of Education, thirty-one weeks in Methods in the Elementary Branches, and twenty weeks in Mental Science, a week being defined as forty-five minutes a day for five days. Practice teaching in a school of children, preceded by fifty periods (of forty-five minutes each) in observation in such school, averaged 131 periods. (Pangburn, 1932, p. 14)

Given the fact that the programs in normal schools usually did not exceed two years and the so-called professional sequence occupied a large segment of the time, the curriculum in normal schools was largely technical, in the sense that Borrowman (1965) defined the term, directly related to skills and knowledge that would be needed in actual teaching:

> Given students with limited knowledge, even of the elementary subject matter they would be required to teach, and a brief period of from six weeks to two years to train them, little could be expected of the normal school. It was perhaps enough to hope that students could be made a master of the elementary-school subjects, given a "bag of tricks"—the more sophisticated title was "the art of teaching"—by means of which his knowledge could be transmitted, and provided with an opportunity to practice his art under supervision. (p. 23)

And the predominant focus on technical education arising primarily from the single-purpose of the normal school contributed to the low professional status of normal school graduates:

> it seems clear that many of the early normal school people were so concerned to create a professional sequence that they largely neglected general education and permitted it to develop chaotically. This lack of carefully planned attention to the general sequence, coupled with an excessively technical concept of the professional sequence, may well have been responsible for the widely cited obsession of teachers with tricks of the trade. (Borrowman, 1956, p. 220)

Therefore, pedagogy, as associated with the normal school legacy, largely focused on the art or the practice of teaching. The term "pedagogy," implying a set of skills or crafts essential for teaching, was associated with the practice—not the theory—of teaching.

Pedagogy as a University Study

Between 1879 and 1890, chairs of pedagogy were established in universities such as Michigan (1879), Wisconsin (1881), Johns Hopkins, Missouri, and North Carolina (1884), Cornell and Indiana (1886), and Clark (1889). By 1890, it was reported that there were chairs of pedagogy in more than 45 universities (Johanningmeier & Johnson, 1975). During the 1890s, California at Berkeley, Minnesota, Nebraska, Northwestern, and Pennsylvania also made appointments for chairs of pedagogy (Brickman, 1986, p. 232; Herbst, 1987, p. 151).

President James B. Angell, in his report to the Board of Trustees in 1874, justified the course of pedagogy in the University of Michigan as follows:

> It cannot be doubted that some instruction in Pedagogics would be very helpful to our Senior class. Many of them are called directly from the University to the management of large schools, some of them to the superintendency of the schools of a town. The whole work of organizing schools, the management of primary and grammar schools, the art of teaching and governing a school—of all this it is desirable that they know something before they go to their new duties. Experience alone can thoroughly train them, but some familiar lectures on these topics would be of essential service to them. (Hinsdale, 1906; in Cohen, 1974, p. 1,414)

As we can see from the above quotation, pedagogy in the university context did not appear to be associated with the practice of teaching. Rather, the concept of pedagogy as conceived in the university setting was more theory- and research-oriented. Toward the end of the nineteenth century, some university scholars began to argue that pedagogy was a legitimate enterprise within the older framework of liberal studies. Borrowman maintained that William Payne, who is widely held as the first incumbent of a chair of pedagogy in an American university, considered pedagogy, as taught in the university, a liberal art or science (Borrowman, 1965, pp. 11–13).

Since one of the most established ideals of an American university is to pursue liberal education (Veysey, 1965), pedagogy as conceived in the university setting tended to alienate itself from the practice of teaching. It was argued that

> even if the work done by the pedagogical chair should pay no immediate attention to the preparation of teachers, it could not fail to be of much practical value. The scientific study and teaching of a science and an art in their purely theoretical aspects always promote the practice of the art; and the presence in every university in the land of pedagogical professor, thoroughly devoted to his chair, could not fail to quicken interest in the subject, and to promote the teaching art. (Hinsdale, 1889; in Cohen, 1974, p. 1,416)

It is clear that pedagogy as conceived in the university setting tried to put on the persona of liberal arts and to move away from the image of practice and art as connected with the normal school tradition. Historically, as were the cases in, for instance, the University of Chicago (White, 1982), the University of Minnesota (Beck, 1980), and the University of Pennsylvania (Brickman, 1986), the department of pedagogy was a part of the liberal arts college and particularly a subdivision of philosophy.

The Discontinuity and Nonconvergence of the Two Traditions of Pedagogy

The Normal School Tradition

With the evolution of normal schools to teachers' colleges to state colleges and then to regional state universities, the normal school lost its identity as a single-purpose institution focused on pedagogy (Goodlad, 1990b; Howey & Zimpher, 1990). The preparation of teachers, once the only mission of these institutions, is now just one of many programs in the multipurpose institution (Cohen, Birnbaum, Pfnister, & Geiger, 1985; Kerr, 1994).

In the process of institutional evolution, normal schools gradually took on an academic or liberal arts orientation (Clifford & Guthrie, 1988, p. 63), and this orientation was not in harmony with the practice- or art-oriented conception of pedagogy. With the lengthening of programs from two years to four years, the liberal arts curriculum occupied more and more time and, therefore, the significance of pedagogy was dramatically reduced.

Pangburn (1932, pp. 33–96) thoroughly studied the curricular development of normal schools as they advanced to collegiate status and found a pattern of curricular expansion and modification based on the model of the four-year curriculum found in universities. The following is her observation:

> A distinctive feature of the development of the teachers college has been the emergence of new curriculum goals in form of degrees and accrediting by institutions of higher learning. The early degrees of the teacher-training schools seemed to indicate a qualitative rather than a

quantitative distinction. They represented the completion of a brief curriculum, usually not exceeding two years of college work. The granting of the Bachelor of Pedagogy and the Master of Pedagogy degrees for the completion of two or three years of college work preceded the granting of the Bachelor of Arts degree and continued side by side with it until about 1920, when the degrees for the shorter courses were discontinued. (p. 95)

It is quite logical that those higher education institutions evolving from normal schools were eager to join the "major league" of established universities and were willing to sever the relationship with the tradition of pedagogy as characterized by normal schools. Therefore, to a great extent, the tradition of pedagogy as associated with normal schools discontinued. It is interesting to note that when Illinois State Normal University, a spearhead in transformation from normal schools to state universities, was granted by the state legislature the privilege to confer degrees in 1907, the Board chose the bachelor of education rather than the bachelor of pedagogy (Harper, 1935, p. 323).

While the pedagogical tradition of normal schools was lost in the evolution from normal schools to state universities, pedagogy as a study in those old prestigious universities suffered the same fate, albeit in a different institutional context and with different manifestations.

The University Tradition

As described in the foregoing, the late nineteenth and early twentieth centuries witnessed a proliferation of chairs of pedagogy in universities. However, the establishment of chairs of pedagogy in universities was not without resistance; many faculty members considered pedagogy—a focus of normal schools—out of the pale of academic respectability. Others believed that pedagogy, while desirable for those intending to teach, should not be allowed to displace any of the liberal arts components of the college curriculum. The opinion was expressed at the 1889 meeting of the New England Association of Colleges and Preparatory Schools that the purpose of colleges was to give a liberal education and that they should not turn aside or fall short of that aim. The pedagogical training, insofar as it was additional to such training, was a handicap to it and liable to infringe upon or diminish liberal education (Pangburn, 1932, p. 23).

Indeed, one of the ideals of a university has been associated with the concept of liberal education. From Kant (1798/1979) to Hutchins (1940), the liberal education ideal has been persistent in the history of higher education. Confronted with the formidable resistance on university campuses, the pedagogical faculty employed the following strategies to maintain a foothold in academia.

The first strategy was to define pedagogy as a liberal study. William Payne (1887) held that pedagogy, as taught in the university, was a liberal art. He insisted that the technical training appropriately offered to immature students in normal schools, who could be expected to become competent craftsmen, was fundamentally different from the liberal education offered to potential educational leaders in the university (Payne, 1887; in Borrowman, 1965, p. 13). Therefore, the emphasis of pedagogy, as conceived by Payne, was on philosophy and history of education, rather than on the method or technique of teaching the young.

The second strategy used by the pedagogical faculty to maintain a foothold in academia was to move away from preparing classroom teachers. When faculty members of pedagogy realized that teaching in lower schools, and especially in elementary schools, was feminized and had a low socioeconomic and professional status, they seized the opportunity to focus on administrative specializations. This was particularly true during the period between 1890 and 1910 when the high school teaching force rose from 9,000 to 42,000 (Powell, 1976). The strategy to move from preparing classroom teachers to preparing administrators could both minimize the conflict with liberal arts faculty, who claimed preparing secondary school teachers was their domain, and enhance the status of pedagogical faculty because administrators had a higher socioeconomic and professional status than teachers did.

Teachers College was a good case in point. Around 1910, Teachers College had curricula preparing its students for 56 distinct educational positions. Students were segregated in training according to their specific vocational destinies (Powell, 1976). This was also the case at the University of Chicago where, under Charles Judd's leadership, his colleagues gradually moved out of the business of preparing teachers and focused on the preparation of its students for administrative and academic positions (White, 1982).

The move away from preparing classroom teachers was also evident for individual pedagogical faculty members who first held university appointments in pedagogy. For example, William Payne, the first American chair of pedagogy, was extolled as one of the pioneers in preparing school administrators (Culbertson, 1988). Paul Hanus moved from a teacher educator to a specialist in school administration during his twenty-year tenure at Harvard. By 1910, Hanus considered himself an expert in school administration (Hazlett, 1989), presumably an expertise of more significance than that in teacher education. It is clear that because professors gradually focused on specializations other than teaching, pedagogy was pushed to the periphery in these ambitious universities.

As associated with the strategies of defining pedagogy as a liberal study and moving away from preparing classroom teachers, the third strategy used by the pedagogical faculty to maintain a foothold in academia was to move beyond the scholarship of pedagogy. The title of Beck's (1980) study of the history of the University of Minnesota College of Education—*Beyond Pedagogy*—captured the essence of the shifted focus in the evolution process. White's (1982) paper, "The decline of the classroom and the Chicago study of education, 1909–1929," also portrayed vividly how Charles Judd and his protégés abolished the laboratory school that John Dewey had established and became committed to a science of education that largely ignored the study of classrooms. Henderson summarized this trend rather well in 1913:

> The introduction of the study into higher education led to new difficulties in regard to the term pedagogy. It was felt to be essentially a normal school subject, concerned especially with the problems of the elementary school and "rule-of-the-thumb" methods of teaching the subjects of its curriculum. Much of this criticism of pedagogy as a university subject had, doubtless, validity, and in consequence it was necessary to modify and expand its content in order to secure for it a permanent foothold and equality of rank. To mark the change there grew up a tendency to substitute the word *education* for *pedagogy* as a title for the department and for professorships. (Henderson, 1913, p. 622)

In other words, by moving from pedagogy to education, faculty members were able to study any topic related to education rather than being confined to the narrow subject of pedagogy. This phenomenon was also indicated in the rapid movement from "Department of Pedagogy" to "School of Education" in the early twentieth century. The University of Wisconsin and the University of Minnesota changed the Department of Pedagogy to the College of Education in 1904 and 1905, respectively (Beck, 1980, pp. 34-35). Ohio State's and Iowa's pedagogy departments became colleges of education in 1907 (Clifford & Guthrie, 1988, p. 64). In Berkeley, a regental authorization in 1889 for instruction in the Art of Teaching led to a two-man Department of Pedagogy in 1892 and then to a School of Education in 1913. At the University of Pennsylvania, the Department of Pedagogy evolved into the School of Education in 1914. As Henderson (p. 622) keenly observed in 1913, "the term 'pedagogy' has to a considerable extent passed out of vogue."

The converging effect of the aforementioned three strategies— defining pedagogy as a liberal study, getting out of the business of preparing teachers, and moving beyond the scholarship of pedagogy—led to the fall of the concept of pedagogy on university campuses. Instead, the all-inclusive concept of education became prevailing and dominant. Nevertheless, although there has been a quest for a science of education starting from the late nineteenth century (Roberts, 1968), a course marked by such well-known figures as Charles Judd, Stanley Hall, and Edward Thorndike, many scholars, such as Josiah Royce (1891/1965), still questioned whether there could be a science of education. The history of the quest for a science of education seemed to put the concept of pedagogy on the periphery rather than in the center. In other words, pedagogy was marginalized.

The rise and fall of the concept of pedagogy is also evident in the degrees of pedagogy conferred by American universities. Rudolph (1977, p. 138) observed that in 1873 programs leading to a Bachelor of Pedagogy and a Bachelor of Didactics were established in Missouri and Iowa, respectively. Table 2.1 displays statistics on how many degrees of pedagogy—including bachelor of pedagogy (B.Ped), master of pedagogy (M.Ped.), and doctor of pedagogy (D.Ped.)— were conferred by American colleges and universities, compiled from the annual reports by the Commissioner of Education over a period of about 25 years.

Table 2.1

Degrees of Pedagogy
Conferred by American Colleges and Universities

Year	B. Ped.	M. Ped.	D. Ped.
1889–1890	54	n / a	n / a
1891–1892	32	32	11
1893–1894	36	n / a	n / a
1895–1896	66	11	6
1897–1898	31	15	5
1899–1900	221	30	5
1901–1902	74	20	11
1903–1904	57	29	3
1905–1906	38	18	n / a
1907–1908	113	n / a	n / a
1909–1910	78	15	1
1911–1912	378	10	3
1913–1914	379	94	6
1915–1916	3	n / a	n / a

Before the 1889–1890 school year, only the following types of degrees were catalogued in the annual reports: letters, science, philosophy, theology, medicine, and law. From 1889–1890 to 1915–1916, pedagogy was listed as a category. However, the degree of Bachelor of Education began to be listed in 1911–1912, and the number of degrees awarded were as follows: 60 for 1911–1912; 113 for 1913–1914, and 720 for 1915–1916. It appears that during the 1910s, the Bachelor of Pedagogy degree was gradually replaced by the Bachelor of Education degree. By 1939–1940, 38,289 Bachelor of Education degrees were conferred in the United States.

Statistics from the annual reports of the Commissioner of Education seem to suggest that Bachelor of Pedagogy degrees had a short history in American colleges and universities and were conferred on a relatively small scale. Master of Pedagogy degrees showed a small but steady increase over the years while Doctor of Pedagogy degrees appeared to be stagnant. When a Doctor of Education degree was established by the Harvard University Graduate School of Education in 1920, it was quickly adopted by many prestigious universities (Eells, 1963, pp. 28-37). Therefore, by the 1920s pedagogy as an earned degree was essentially eliminated from American colleges and universities, an observation which is consistent with Henderson's statement that the term pedagogy was increasingly out of vogue when he wrote the entry of pedagogy for *A Cyclopedia of Education* in 1913.

It is perhaps appropriate here to go beyond the American context and make two comments on the study of pedagogy from an international perspective. First, an examination of the programs listed in *Higher Education in the European Community: Student Handbook* (Mohr, 1990) reveals that pedagogy or pedagogics is used to denote the relevant programs in the former Federal Republic of Germany, Denmark, Greece, Italy, and the Netherlands, while education or educational science is used in Spain, France, Ireland, Portugal, and the UK. It would be interesting to inquire into whether this represents a linguistic and/or conceptual difference. Second, the neglect of pedagogy is also lamented by Brian Simon, the well-known British historian, in his article entitled "Why no pedagogy in England?" (Simon, 1981/1985). The reason does not seem to be different from that in the United States. As Simon (1983/1994, p. 142) observed, "As educational studies became more rigorous and inevitably academic, the historic neglect of pedagogy was accentuated."

Three Orientations to Pedagogy

As the analyses in the foregoing show, the two traditions of pedagogy were discontinued before they converged. The normal school and the university traditions were lost in different institutional contexts but for a similar reason—moving beyond pedagogy and in pursuit of something more prestigious. The result of the failure to converge has been detrimental to the education of school teachers. There has been no coherent model combining the two traditions of pedagogy for the education of teachers, and therefore, there has been no sound concept of pedagogy underlying the education of teachers.

Su's (1986) review indicated that teacher education reform in the United States between 1890 and 1986 was replete with chronic issues and recurring themes regarding how to educate teachers. The fundamental difficulty underlying these issues and themes is how to define what teaching entails, and how to prepare teachers accordingly.

Since there is no unified concept of pedagogy that retains a balance between the art and science of teaching, pedagogy has not been employed as a vital concept to capture the essence of the education of teachers. Rather, in the practice of preparing teachers, there are some fragmented views regarding what teaching entails and how teachers should be educated, and I refer to these views as "orientations to pedagogy." The following is an account of the three orientations to pedagogy.

Subject Matter as Pedagogy

This notion of subject matter as pedagogy has a long history. Before the normal schools were established in the middle of the nineteenth century, teachers for lower schools were educated under the notion of subject matter as pedagogy. The assumption is that since what teaching entails is the mastery of subject matter, subject matter per se is pedagogy.

This notion, underlying the Master of Arts in Teaching (MAT) programs, has strong support in the arts and sciences departments in universities. Some well-known scholars in arts and sciences deny the need for professional education for teachers. For example, Robert M. Hutchins is a case in point. Hutchins (1940, p. 147) claimed that "all there is to teaching can be learned through a good education and being a teacher." Bestor (1985, p. 147) made a similar comment:

> A new curriculum for the education of teachers, based firmly upon the liberal arts and sciences, rather than upon the mere vocational skills of pedagogy, will do more to restore the repute of the public schools than any other step that can be taken. Not only will teachers be adequately trained in the disciplines they undertake to teach, they will also be imbued with respect for those disciplines and will be prepared to resist the anti-intellectualism that currently threatens the schools. Under a well-ordered plan, the gateway to teaching will be the gateway of learning itself.

Not only faculty members in arts and sciences, but also some scholars in education hold the notion of subject matter as pedagogy. Recently, Kerr (1983) and Kramer (1991) make the following arguments:

A state might, for example, certify graduates to teach who score in the top 10 percent on the National Teacher Examination, and who subsequently have, through a state arrangement, done an internship in the schools. Thus, the brightest who might consider teaching were it not for the requirement of taking education courses could circumvent that obstacle. (Kerr, 1983, p. 546)

How to teach English literature should be the concern of professors of English, not experts in curriculum and instruction. The methodology can best be integrated with the subject itself, with the subject as the main focus, not the methodology. Everything you need to know about how to teach English—that can be taught didactically—can be learned within the framework of an undergraduate English major. (Kramer, 1991, p. 219)

In the same vein, Kramer characterizes a method course as gimmicky. The notion of subject matter as pedagogy is clear in Kerr's and Kramer's arguments. Generally speaking, much of the rhetoric that teachers are not well prepared in subject matter also implicitly expresses the notion of subject matter as pedagogy.

Subject Matter and Pedagogy as Separate Identities

That subject matter and pedagogy have separate identities is the dominant notion underlying the preparation of school teachers. Su (1986, p. 29) commented that teacher education programs in the U.S. have not changed much from the four components proposed by Russell in 1900: general culture or liberal education, special scholarship or subject studies, professional knowledge, and technical skills. It appears that the first two components fall into the category of subject matter and the last two into pedagogy, a dichotomy illustrating the separation between subject matter and pedagogy.

If subject matter is relatively less controversial, what constitutes pedagogy is a topic for on-going debate and is always in flux. William Bennett's remark at the National Governors' Association—"Teachers should demonstrate competence in their subject area, have good character, and have the interest and ability to communicate with young people" (Clifford & Guthrie, 1988, p. 16)—is usually criticized for his neglect of pedagogy, which is traditionally conceived as professional training in schools of education and lower schools.

This criticism might be unjustified because Bennett's remarks fit in perfectly with the model of subject matter plus pedagogy, and pedagogy is defined by him as "good character" and "the interest and ability to communicate with young people." Even the saying that "Great teachers are born, not made" implies the orientation of subject matter plus pedagogy, with pedagogy being defined as a gift or a natural endowment.

What constitutes pedagogy has been an issue of debate in the history of the education of educators. In the 1929 *Commonwealth Teacher-Training Study*, Charters and Waples (1929, pp. 14–16) identified "a list of twenty-five traits judged by competent critics of teachers to be most important." This list contained the following:

> 1. adaptability; 2. attractiveness, personal appearance; 3. breadth of interest; 4. carefulness; 5. considerateness; 6. co-operation; 7. dependability; 8. enthusiasm; 9. fluency; 10. forcefulness; 11. good judgment; 12. health; 13. honesty; 14. industry; 15. leadership; 16. magnetism; 17. neatness; 18. open-mindedness; 19. originality; 20. progressiveness; 21. promptness; 22. refinement; 23. scholarship; 24. self-control; and 25. thrift.

In this long list, only item 23, "scholarship"—which was defined as "the sum of the mental attainment of a scholar; scholarly character or qualities; learning; erudition" (p. 60)—is associated with the concept of subject matter knowledge; all other items are basically personal characteristics. This represents the *humanistic* approach to pedagogy. This approach continues in more recent research. For example, in the 1960s and 1970s, there were some studies on teachers' warmth and other personal characteristics as reviewed by Dunkin and Biddle (1974) and Shulman (1986).

There is also the *behaviorist* approach to pedagogy. The 1929 *Commonwealth Teacher-Training Study* also listed 1,010 activities that were grouped under the following six categories: instruction, management, extra classroom activities, administrative relation, personal and professional advancement, and activities concerning supplies and plant. Although it is often criticized as trivial, "this study [The 1929 Commonwealth Teacher-Training Study] still stands today as perhaps the only comprehensive and objective effort to provide a functional basis for pedagogical education" (Smith, 1980, p. 1). This behaviorist approach continues later on. As illustrated in Borg's

(1972) article entitled "The minicourse as a vehicle for changing teaching behavior," the microteaching movement in the late 1960s and 1970s focused on changing teaching behaviors. Proficiency- or competency-based teacher education in the 1970s established behaviors as objectives and used these prespecified objectives as criteria in assessing student progress toward teaching competence (e.g., Andersen, 1973; Houston & Howsam, 1972; Rosner, 1972). Sarason (1978–1979, p. 3) captured the essence of competency-based teacher education by making the following comment:

> The less flattering characterization of CBTE [competency-based teacher education] likens it to task analysis through time-and-motion studies of factory workers made famous by Taylor early in this century. This characterization complains about the narrowness of view that CBTE promotes: "Competency-based programs ignore or deemphasize the social, interactional, and hierarchical aspects of work in a school or school system."

Generally speaking, this behaviorist approach to pedagogy reduces teaching to simple behaviors and is associated with the technification of teaching, an idea that suggests teaching is an applied science and tends to drive the value dimension out of teaching and teacher education (Dill, 1990; Goodlad, 1994c; Goodlad, Soder, & Sirotnik, 1990; Ryan, 1987; Sirotnik, 1990; Strike, Haller, & Soltis, 1988; Strike & Soltis, 1985).

Subject Matter and Pedagogy as Both Separate and Overlapped Identities

Since the 1980s there has been a tendency to develop knowledge-based teacher education. After reviewing reports from the 1929 *Commonwealth Teacher-Training Study* to the 1976 *Report of the Bicentennial Commission on Education for the Profession of Teaching*, Smith (1980) made three major comments, with two of them being the following:

> The second thing these surveys and movements share is the failure to give primary consideration to the knowledge base of pedagogical education. The third similarity among these studies of pedagogical education is that, while they all recognize the necessity of skill

development, none gave an analysis of how pedagogical knowledge provides a basis for such development. (p. 4)

Smith held that pedagogical knowledge consists of two types—clinical and academic:

> Clinical knowledge is that which teachers use as they help students, either individually or in groups. It is the verbal counterpart of pedagogical behavior, and is expressed as definitions, principles, facts, and values. It is used as teachers give instruction in the performance of a skill such as giving feedback, asking contrary to fact questions, making diagnoses or other judgments.
>
> Academic pedagogical knowledge consists of the definitions, principles, facts, and values that comprise the content of educational history, philosophy, sociology, psychology, and so on. It is used mainly in developing and justifying educational policies and programs. (p. 64)

Smith proposed these two types of pedagogical knowledge on the basis of logical classification. In contrast, Shulman and his colleagues embarked on a journey to empirically inquire into teachers' knowledge. Grossman (1990, p. 5), one of Shulman's students, conceptualized teachers' knowledge in Figure 2.1.

Based on this conceptualization, Grossman (1990) inquired into how beginning secondary English teachers with or without teacher education differ in their approaches to teaching and how those with or without training in pedagogical content knowledge vary in their teaching.

Shulman and his colleagues' work differs from the previous orientations of pedagogy in two important aspects. First, they try to conceptualize the knowledge base of teaching, and to argue—by conducting empirical studies on neophyte and experienced teachers in different subjects—that teaching is fundamentally a process of comprehension, reasoning, transformation, and reflection. For example, Shulman (1987, p. 15) proposed the following model of pedagogical reasoning and action:

Figure 2.1

Model of Teacher Knowledge

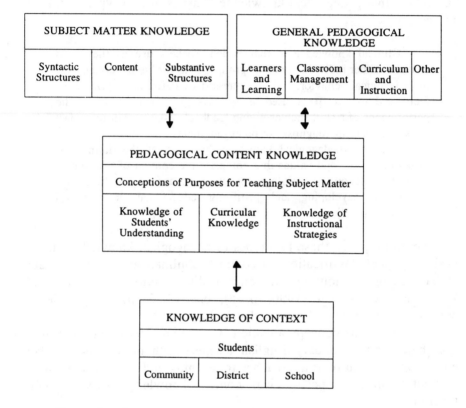

Comprehension
Of purposes, subject matter structures, ideas within and outside the discipline

Transformation
Preparation: critical interpretation and analysis of texts, structuring and segmenting, development of a curricular repertoire, and clarification of purposes
Presentation: use of a representational repertoire which includes analogies, metaphors, examples, demonstrations, explanations, and so forth
Selection: choice from among an instructional repertoire which includes modes of teaching, organizing, managing, and arranging

Adaptation and Tailoring to Student Characteristics: consideration of conceptions, preconceptions, misconceptions, and difficulties, language, culture, and motivations, social class, gender, age, ability, aptitude, interests, self concepts, and attention

Instruction
Management, presentations, interactions, group work, discipline, humor, questioning, and other aspects of active teaching, discovery or inquiry instruction, and the observable forms of classroom teaching

Evaluation
Checking for student understanding during interactive teaching
Testing student understanding at the end of lessons or units
Evaluating one's own performance, and adjusting for experiences

Reflection
Reviewing, reconstructing, reenacting and critically analyzing one's own and the class's performance, and grounding explanations in evidence

New Comprehensions
Of purposes, subject matter, students, teaching, and self
Consolidation of new understandings, and learnings from experience

It is clear that Shulman and his colleagues endeavor to go beyond the humanistic and behaviorist approaches to pedagogy and toward the *cognitive* approach to pedagogy, an endeavor which is evident in Grossman's (1990, p. 4) observation of the shift from research on teacher behavior and student achievement to studying teachers' cognitive processes, which include their thoughts, judgments, decisions, and plans, and to the efforts to describe and delineate the knowledge base of teaching.

The second difference between previous views and Shulman's conceptions of pedagogy is the notion of pedagogical content knowledge. Although the notion is not totally new because Dewey (1904) and Kerr (1987) discussed the importance for teachers to "psychologize," "humanize," and "interpret" subject matter in teaching, it is Shulman and his colleagues who clearly defined the concept of pedagogical content knowledge.

The concept of pedagogical content knowledge not only adds a new and important dimension to the concept of pedagogy, but it also establishes the connection between subject matter and pedagogy. Therefore, subject matter *per se* is not the whole of pedagogy. Neither are subject matter and pedagogy completely separate. Rather, they overlap. This notion of overlap not only provides a new perspective to resurrect and justify the concept of pedagogy, but also mandates the "joint work" (Grossman, 1994) between faculties in the arts and sciences and in education to develop prospective teachers' understandings of subject matter knowledge and pedagogical content knowledge.

To summarize the discussions on the evolution of the orientations to pedagogy, there seems to be two major themes: first, the evolution from the humanistic and behaviorist approaches to the cognitive approach; second, from subject matter as pedagogy and total separation of subject matter from pedagogy to an integrative notion regarding the relationship between subject matter and pedagogy.

The Relationship between Science and Art in Pedagogy

Pedagogy is usually defined as the science and art of teaching. However, answers to questions such as what is science and what is the relationship between art and science in pedagogy are not clear.

To isolate teachers' personal characteristics and emphasize their effects on teaching assumes that the art of teaching is largely a function of personal characteristics and that the science and art of teaching are, to a great extent, dissociated from each other. The saying that "teachers are born rather than made" also assumes that teaching is largely a function of innate characteristics. This saying implies that if there is a science in pedagogy, science and art are, to a great extent, not related; and that the art of teaching is primarily a function of personal characteristics.

Gage, in his seminal work *The Scientific Basis of the Art of Teaching* (1979), distinguished between a science of teaching and a scientific basis for the art of teaching. He argued that the idea of a science of teaching is erroneous because it implies that good teaching will someday be attainable by closely following rigorous laws that yield high predictability and control much as chemists use laws to obtain predictable results. Rather, he argued that teaching is essentially a form of art that is based on science:

Scientific method can contribute relationships between variables taken two at a time and when, in the form of interactions, three or perhaps four or more at a time. Beyond say four, the usefulness of what science can give the teacher begins to weaken, because teachers cannot apply, at least not without help and not on the run, the more complex interactions. At this point, the teacher as an artist must step in and make clinical, or artistic judgments about the best ways to teach. (p. 20)

Therefore, Gage's notion of the relationship between science and art in pedagogy is well illustrated in the title of his book—*The Scientific Basis of the Art of Teaching*—i.e., there is a hierarchical relationship between science and art in teaching, with science being foundational and secondary and art being the ultimate and primary.

As to the notion of scientific basis, Gage understands it in a positivist sense when he observes that "the scientific base for the art of teaching will consist of two-variable relationships and lower-order interactions. The higher-order interactions between four and more variables must be handled by the teacher as artist" (p. 20). Throughout his book, Gage reviewed empirical studies that inquired into the relationship between teachers' characteristics, such as attitude and behavior, and students' characteristics, such as attitude and academic achievement.

Therefore, Gage probably would not define pedagogy as the science and art of teaching because he denies the existence of a science of teaching. Rather, his definition is probably close to "pedagogy is an art which has an empirically verifiable, scientific basis"—a definition, as mentioned in the foregoing, stipulating a hierarchical relationship between art and science.

Although Gage argues eloquently that teaching has a scientific basis, teaching also has a normative basis. Teaching is embedded in value judgments. Goodlad (1994c) raised, in his *What Schools Are For*, the issue of what schools are doing, are expected to do, and should do. There is always some tension between these three levels of questions, and the perceived tension influences what teachers do in classroom teaching. Teaching is such a value laden enterprise—as illustrated by Strike and Soltis (1985), Strike, Haller, and Soltis (1988), Dill (1990), and Goodlad, Soder, and Sirotnik (1990)—that when a teaching practice is justified, it usually resorts to both empirical findings and value judgments, a point which was put forth persuasively by Paul Hirst (1966). In more cases than not, empirical findings are only meaningful when they are consistent with value judgments. In other words, value judgments become the sifter for assimilating empirical findings. Therefore, the art of teaching has both a scientific and a normative base.

There has been a trend to technificate teaching to the degree of ignoring the normative basis of the art of teaching, and grounding teaching solely on empirical findings (Ryan, 1987). The result of this technification does not improve the professional status of teaching. Rather, it ignores the richness and complexity associated with teaching and erodes the very foundation of educating teachers (Sirotnik, 1990).

Pedagogy and Professional Status of Teaching

Whether teaching is a profession and if not, how to achieve professional status, has been one of the foci of educational debate. There have been many proposals to attain or improve the professional status of teaching, such as raising teachers' salaries, improving teachers' working conditions, empowering teachers, raising entry level requirements for teacher education programs, lengthening the programs, and grounding teaching on a moral basis. Nonetheless, there seems to be confusion between the cause and effect of professionalizing teaching. Many of the proposals for profession-alizing teaching appear to be effects rather than causes. Furthermore, as Soder (1990a, 1991) persuasively argued, what is a profession, what is teaching, and how we should ground the argument for the professional status of teaching are among the issues that need to be addressed.

It appears that the lack of a coherent orientation to pedagogy, as illustrated in the foregoing, is one of the culprits for the low status of teaching. If we, as educators of educators, are unable to convincingly argue what teaching entails, which is the very essence of the concept of pedagogy, then we will not be able to persuasively define what we do, and by default, we will be defined by others. This is perhaps one of the reasons why the concept of pedagogy has been resurrected in recent years to argue for the nature of teaching. Nonetheless, given the fact that there has not been a coherent concept of pedagogy, to simply invoke the concept will not help us improve teaching and teacher education.

There are mainly three approaches to resurrecting and strengthening the concept of pedagogy. The first approach is to integrate ideas as manifested in the evolution of the concept of pedagogy and thus establish a more coherent concept of pedagogy. In history, orientations to pedagogy gradually evolved from the humanistic and behaviorist approaches to the cognitive approach, and from subject matter as pedagogy and total separation of subject matter from pedagogy to an integrative notion regarding the relationship between subject matter and pedagogy. The relationship between the science and the art of teaching evolved from treating the science and the art as two parallel parts to a more hierarchical notion, with pedagogy being ultimately a form of art that has a solid basis. Furthermore, the basis of the art is both scientific and normative. This integrative concept of pedagogy moves beyond the one-sidedness and superficiality as displayed in its evolution and provides a solid base for designing teacher education programs and improving teaching.

The second approach to resurrecting and strengthening the concept of pedagogy is to ensure the status of pedagogy from an organizational standpoint. As Goodlad (1990b, 1994a) argued for the Center for Pedagogy, work related to pedagogy should have its distinctive organizational structure and protected budget on university campuses. Otherwise, work related to pedagogy will be subject to whims. In relation to the organizational structure, work related to pedagogy should also be rewarded according to the very nature of the work. Furthermore, because of the integrative nature of the concept of pedagogy, the Center of Pedagogy is a tripartite entity consisting of faculty members from arts and sciences, pedagogy, and lower schools, a notion which was put forth by Goodlad (1994a).

However, the integrative conception for pedagogy, the organizational structure, and the protected budget are necessary but not sufficient conditions for upholding the concept of pedagogy. The third approach to resurrecting and strengthening pedagogy is to fortify the normative and scientific bases of teaching. As to the normative base, the moral dimensions of teaching should be emphasized. As Soder (1990a, 1991) observed, if we base the practice of teaching only on subject matter and pedagogical knowledge, then what teachers do will be equivalent to that of a "lackey." Because children are compelled and defenseless, teaching has moral obligations and thus moral praiseworthiness.

As to the scientific base of the practice of teaching, a brief review of the tradition of pedagogy in university settings revealed that the development of educational research moved quickly from pedagogical to educational issues. Much of the work in the realm of educational research has been developed in the area where education and other disciplines intersect. In other words, much of the research work in schools of education could be conducted by researchers in other areas. This is why there is educational philosophy, educational psychology, educational sociology, educational history, educational anthropology, etc. Although it is constructive to develop knowledge in relation to many other disciplines and areas, education as a research area forgets, to a great extent, its *raison d'être*—i.e., to improve teaching and learning in lower schools. After all, wonderful work in, for instance, educational philosophy, educational psychology, and educational sociology is still philosophical, psychological, and sociological in nature. As Gage observed (1979, p. 93):

> We should, of course, look for indirect help from research on cognitive development, the reading process, the brain and neural processes, cultural pluralism, school environments, and other matters only obliquely related to ways of teaching. But we should also not hesitate to look straight at the problems of teaching.

In short, the pursuit of pedagogical work—the distinctive nature of the school of education—should be the hallmark of the school of education. For so many years, the school of education has been permeated by the values and conducts of liberal arts faculty. It is now time to reorient the school of education to the concept of pedagogy.

The above three approaches—having an integrative notion of pedagogy, securing an identifiable organizational structure and protected budget for the work related to pedagogy, and strengthening the scientific and normative bases of teaching—are interconnected and interdependent. None of them will be sufficient for strengthening and resurrecting the concept of pedagogy. A combination of the three strategies offers the best chance for success.

Summary

The purpose of this chapter is to place the current resurrection of the concept of pedagogy in a historical context. What we have learned is that the two traditions of pedagogy—with almost exclusive emphasis on the artistic and theoretical aspects of teaching—did not converge, a fact which resulted in no coherent conception of pedagogy. However, the connotations or elements of the concept of pedagogy continue to evolve. It is now time to integrate these elements and to resurrect and strengthen the concept of pedagogy as the hallmark of the school of education.

When John Dewey (1896), in a letter to the board of trustees, argued passionately for the establishment of the Department of Pedagogy at the University of Chicago, he wrote that "the whole primary and secondary staff ... are being left unduly to the mercy of accident, caprice, routine or useless experiment from lack of scientific training [in the Department of Pedagogy]." Therefore, Dewey held that the purpose of the Department of Pedagogy is, in his own words, to provide the young with "as nearly as possible an ideal education." It is now time to heed Dewey's thesis made almost a century ago and to make pedagogy the focus of our work.

CHAPTER THREE

The Education Faculty and Their Status

As discussed in the second chapter, the education professoriate in those elite universities emerged out of the need for practical functions such as educating teachers rather than conducting research. Therefore, the school of education and its faculty had a low status in those elite universities from the very beginning. As to the school of education in regional state universities, the opinion that "once a normal school, always a normal school" prevails. Thus, the school of education and its faculty, as Ducharme and Agne (1986) summarized, are among the least welcome guests in the establishment of higher education. As a matter of fact, in the history of education, serious questions about whether the school of education and its faculty belong to academia were raised several times by well-known and influential scholars such as Abraham Flexner (1930) and Robert Hutchins (1940).

Status indicates the location of an entity in a hierarchy. When a shortage of resources arises, it is usually the low-status entity that is hurt first. The higher the status an entity enjoys, the fitter it is for survival. Therefore, status is always among the foci of people's attention. Soder (1989b, p. 1) summarized the importance and ubiquity of the concept of status:

Cain slays Abel over a status issue. Achilles battles Agamemnon (and, perhaps, himself) over issues of status. The creation of a Round Table resolves for Arthur's knights an issue of status. A potlatch resolves at least temporarily issues of status for a Kwakiutl chief. These actions across remote time and space make sense to us because we know—at least tacitly—what is at stake. The knight of the round table would understand our battles for a corner office with four windows and a Mondrian on the wall.

A century has passed since the inception of the school of education, but the status of the school of education and its faculty is still an issue. In this chapter, I will first discuss some quantitative data regarding the background of the education faculty and their perceptions of the status of the school of education. I will then use qualitative data from interviews to describe the themes related to the status issue. Finally I will discuss the implications of these findings.

Background of the Education Faculty

Of the 948 tenure-line faculty members in the sample (please see the appendix for a detailed description of the sample), 50% had the Ph.D. and 31% possessed the Ed.D. Therefore, many education faculty did not have terminal degrees. It is commonly perceived that the Ph.D. is a research-oriented degree while the Ed.D. is a more practice-oriented one, although in many cases whether doctoral candidates receive a Ph.D. or an Ed.D. depends on the institutions and programs from which they graduated. Nonetheless, because of the common perception in academia, the Ph.D. is more valued than the Ed.D. Judged by this common—but often misleading—perception, only about half of the education faculty have the Ph.D., the widely recognized degree for academia. Therefore, those faculty members in the arts and sciences might feel that the education faculty are of a lower status because of their training.

Generally speaking, within the community of education faculty, those in research universities enjoy a higher status than those in, for example, comprehensive universities. The percentage of Ph.D. holders in the sample varied from 56% for research universities to 54% for doctorate granting universities, 41% for comprehensive universities, and 47% for liberal arts colleges. There appears to be a positive association between the percentage of Ph.D. holders and the status of the faculty group.

Across all types of higher education institutions, only 12% of the sample did not possess a credential or certificate for teaching, service, or administration of lower schools; and the percentage decreased from research universities (17%) to doctorate granting universities (12%) and to comprehensive universities (6%), but increased again for liberal arts colleges (13%). Both research universities and liberal arts colleges had high percentages of those who did not have certificates for lower schools, but perhaps for different reasons. In research universities, it is because there are more research-oriented faculty members. In liberal arts colleges, it is because there are more liberal arts faculty who are involved in teacher education. Both the research-oriented education faculty and the liberal arts faculty tend not to have certificates for the lower schools.

The credentials most commonly held by the education faculty were secondary (58%) and elementary teaching certificates (37%). Other credentials held by the faculty in the school of education included principal certification (15%), special education certification (10%), superintendent certification (8%), counselor certification (8%), program administrator certification (7%), and school psychologist certification (5%).

Most of the education faculty had experience in lower schools. Of the sample, 71% had at least some experience teaching in elementary schools and 28% had experience of more than 11 years. Of the sample, 82% had at least some experience teaching in secondary schools, and 11% had experience of more than 11 years. Only about 18% of the sample did not have any experience either in elementary or secondary schools. Therefore, the majority of the education faculty have experience in lower schools. Since the culture in the lower schools is quite different from that in academia, it could be hypothesized that the experience that the educational faculty have in lower schools might add to the tension between the arts and sciences faculty and the education faculty.

Of the sample, 31% did not teach and supervise students in the teacher education program within the last three years. As expected, the percentages of those who were not involved in teacher education decreased from research universities (36%), to doctorate granting universities (32%), to comprehensive universities (26%), and to liberal arts colleges (3%). It is surprising to observe that even in comprehensive universities—the type of higher education institutions that educate a majority of our teachers—26% of the faculty were not involved in teacher education in the three years prior to the survey. It appears that the mission of the education faculty, except for those in the liberal arts colleges, has indeed become diversified.

The demographic data about the education faculty illustrate some of their unique characteristics in comparison to the arts and sciences faculty. About a third of the education faculty have the Ed.D., the terminal degree in education, rather than the widely recognized terminal degree (Ph.D.) for academia. A majority of the education faculty members are certified to work in lower schools, and many of them have much experience in lower schools. The work experience of the education faculty might be a source of the cultural difference between the education faculty and those in arts and sciences. The education faculty's academic training and work experience in lower schools appear to be among the factors contributing to the lower status of the school of education. It is interesting to note that the education faculty in research universities, who enjoy higher status among the education faculty, have a higher percentage of Ph.D. holders, are less likely to have credentials for lower schools, and are less involved in teacher education.

The Status of the School of Education and Its Teacher Education Program

The Status of the School of Education

Academic rigor is a very important factor in determining the status of an academic unit. Usually an academic unit with less academic rigor in admission, course work, and graduation is unlikely to enjoy a high status. The respondents of the survey were asked to rate the academic rigor of the school of education in relation to other schools and departments. Of the sample, 34% indicated that the school of education was "more rigorous" than others, 60% selected "no more or less rigorous," and only 6% chose "more rigorous." It is clear that the education faculty tend to perceive the academic rigor of the school of education to be less than other schools and departments.

The percentage of the education faculty perceiving the school of education as less academically rigorous decreased from research universities to liberal arts colleges. It was 37% for research universities, 35% for doctorate granting universities, 30% for comprehensive universities, and 31% for liberal arts colleges. It is interesting to note that although the education faculty in research universities enjoy a higher status than those from other universities, schools of education in research universities are perceived to be less academically rigorous than their counterparts in other universities. Therefore, there is a negative association between the status within the community of the education faculty and the status within the university.

The Academic Rigor of the Teacher Education Program

The respondents were also asked to rate the academic rigor of the courses of the teacher education program as compared to those outside the school of education. Of the sample, 31% indicated courses in the teacher education program were academically "less rigorous" than those outside of the school of education; 63% chose "no more or less rigorous;" and only 6% selected "more rigorous." The percentages of faculty who selected "less rigorous" varied for different types of institutions—34% for research universities, 37% for doctorate granting universities, 25% for comprehensive universities, and 11% for liberal arts colleges. On the other side of the same coin, the percentage of faculty perceiving teacher education courses as more rigorous than those outside the school of education increased from 4% in research universities and 3% in doctorate granting universities, to 10% in comprehensive universities and to 21% in liberal arts colleges. The pattern in the percentages seems to indicate that teacher education has a higher status in comprehensive universities and liberal arts colleges than in research and doctorate granting universities.

The respondents were also asked to respond to the following question: "How do you think most of the faculty *outside this SCDE* [school, college, and department of education] would rate the academic rigor of the *teacher education courses?*" Of the sample, 74% selected "less rigorous," 25% "no more or less rigorous," and only 2% "more rigorous." Again the percentage varied for faculty in different types of higher education institutions. Eighty-four percent of those in research universities and 80% in doctorate granting universities selected "less rigorous," while the corresponding percentages for those in comprehensive and liberal arts colleges were 58% and 71%, respectively. Therefore, comparatively speaking, the faculty in comprehensive universities and liberal arts colleges felt more comfortable about the academic rigor of teacher education courses than their counterparts in research and doctorate granting universities.

The aforementioned data illustrate the following patterns as to the status of the school of education, in general, and teacher education, in particular. First, the school of education is perceived to be academically less rigorous than other departments and schools. Second, 31% of the education faculty perceive that teacher education courses are less rigorous than those outside the school of education, while 74% of the education faculty indicate that those outside of education would feel teacher education courses are less rigorous. Therefore, teacher education has a low status within the school of education, but a much lower status in the university. Third, the education faculty in comprehensive universities and liberal arts colleges feel more comfortable about the status of their schools of education and teacher education programs than their counterparts in research and doctorate granting universities.

Status of the School of Education and Teacher Education as Reflected in Qualitative Interview Data

Generally speaking, the school of education has a lower status in the university, a statement that applies to every type of higher education institution—from large public flagship research universities to small liberal arts colleges. The following are excerpts of interview data from the faculty members:

Status? Pass the toilet paper. (Professor, public research university)

I'm in the faculty senate. I see the intellectual bigotry against educators. (Assistant Professor, public doctorate granting university)

We fight with home ec to see who is going to be at the bottom of the heap. (Associate professor, public doctorate granting university)

Education and home ec are on the bottom. Arts and Sciences look down on us. (Professor, public doctorate granting university)

They look down on us as a trade school. (Professor, public comprehensive university)

The order is Arts and Science—as far as they're concerned, they're the only college—then business, nursing, education. (Professor, public comprehensive university)

The A&S people think they are vastly superior. But prejudice against education has always been strong. When I was initiated into Phi Beta Kappa, I was the first person from education to be so in my school or area. At the dinner just prior to the initiation, an acquaintance took me aside and, not knowing that it was going to be me, said, "Can you believe that we are initiating somebody from education?" (Professor, public comprehensive university)

You know about the widest street in the world? Columbia? Well, it's the same old story. Not that obvious here as it was at Columbia. It's still here. (Professor, public comprehensive university)

Status is low. It's like at [another Private Research/Doctorate Granting University] education just sort of pulsates there. (Professor, private research/doctorate granting university)

Status is the same as everywhere else. Education is low. I'm doing fine myself. You can work with some of them. I do. I've been around here for such a long time that they make comments to me about how bad the education people are without realizing I'm in education. (Professor, private research/doctorate granting university)

The normal prejudices with regard to education are apparent here. (Professor, private liberal arts college)

There is a feeling on the part of the faculty that the status or role of the school of education continues to diminish. This is particularly true in those universities that are moving from regional to national status:

This place was primarily teacher ed. Now business, the MBAs, creative arts, sciences are all coming on strong. (Professor, public comprehensive university)

There's less going to education. Others are looking at education as a smaller and smaller fraction of the overall action. Business and computer science are the biggies. Economics, too. Engineering's another hot area. They hire at different salaries. (Associate Professor, public comprehensive university)

Arts and sciences think we're second class citizens. Medicine and business are so separate they don't have any interaction with us. I think they wonder why we are in the education business. They want to make [the institution] a world-class university, so they look to English, medicine, areas of strength. They don't have negative feelings toward education—they just overlook us. (Professor, private comprehensive university)

The education faculty resent the low and diminishing status of the school of education. Some feel that the perceived inferiority of the education faculty is not justified; some indicate that the arts and sciences are dependent upon the enrollment of the school of education; still others point out that the power structure of the university renders the school of education a low status:

The English Department is out to gain control. We have people who have equal or superior credentials. They don't know anything—they're 40 years behind the time. (Professor, public comprehensive university)

Arts and sciences say they depend on us for students—which indeed they do—but they expect us to do all the recruiting. But they'll never let you forget that they are the ones upholding the academic standards, and they'll let us know whenever we're slipping. They're leeches. They're leeching on us. (Professor, public comprehensive university)

There is a strong resentment of business. When enrollment in education was declining, they thought they could save things by pushing business. (Professor, public comprehensive university)

Business, liberal arts have assumed leadership positions. Because of
the turnover of deans, we haven't had a strong advocate at the
university level. (Professor, public doctorate granting university)

The aforementioned interview data indicate that the school of
education has a low and diminishing status in the university. It is
disturbing to note from the interview data that within the school of
education, teacher education has even a lower status.

Education is the bastard child here, especially teacher education.
(Professor, private research/doctorate granting university)

One division thinks teacher ed is the center of life; the other divisions
think teacher ed is minor. (Professor, private research/doctorate
granting university)

Like on many campuses, we're seen as second rate by those in liberal
arts. Preparing teachers is low priority for them. (Professor, public
comprehensive university)

The status of teacher ed here? If there were a room below the
basement, that's where teacher ed would be. It's that bad. When I first
came here, there were a lot of joint appointments between education
and the liberal arts. That all fizzled—they've all disappeared. The last
ten years, all we've been doing is taking potshots at each other, you
know, what with enrollments going down. The paucity of students
created the problem; going into commerce and engineering. There was
lots of competition for resources; things got pretty nasty. Right now,
we've got a proposal we're working on with some people over there
in liberal arts; first time, I'd say, in maybe eight years. Everybody's
still in their caves. (Professor, public research university)

In instances where teacher education has a relatively high status
in a school of education, the reasons given for the high status are
related to the fact that teacher education is treated as a cash cow. The
reasons are not related to the quality of teacher education, the
emphasis on teacher education, the moral responsibility of the
university to educate teachers, or the inherent nature of teacher
education:

Teacher education is more prominent right now because of increasing enrollments. But that can change. (Professor, public doctorate granting university)

Education is very low compared to liberal arts and other professional programs. Teacher education status is going up—people are beginning to realize that if we didn't have a teacher ed program, we wouldn't exist as a college. (Professor, private research/doctorate granting university)

The teacher education program is about all there is—it's by far the most important. (Professor, public comprehensive university)

Status is low, but it varies with demand for teachers, so it's starting to edge up a bit. It was music, physical education, A&S. Now it's business. (Professor, public comprehensive university)

[In speaking of interviewee's overall institution] They've never gotten into an enrollment crunch, so they've never had to fight over bodies. (Assistant Professor, private liberal arts colleges)

During the interviews, faculty members suggested that the school of education and teacher education are trapped at the lower level of the hierarchy within the university. In other words, the low status of the school of education, in general, and teacher education, in particular, seem to be institutionalized in universities and colleges:

The arts and sciences people will not accept any of the education courses for credit in fulfilling core requirements. (Professor, private research/doctorate granting university)

The university is ambivalent about teacher education. They pay lip service, but that's all. We wanted to raise the minimum GPA to get in. The university said no—they wanted to keep this place to dump students. (Professor, public research university)

The interview data also reveal education faculty members' perceptions as to why the school of education has a low status. The most common reason is that education is less rigorous than arts and sciences. In other words, what is taught in education classes and particularly teacher education classes is considered "Mickey Mouse."

Status? The typical bias is evident. The lesser worth of what we do. Liberal arts faculty feel we aren't as rigorous or as worthy. Students feel the same way. (Assistant Professor, private liberal arts college)

The status is low. You want *prima facie* evidence? Professors don't have to take methods classes, nobody had to train them to be teachers. Even the language is different. If you're a professor, you say, "I have to meet my class now." (Associate Professor, private research/ doctorate granting university)

The liberal arts people think we're Mickey Mouse. (Professor, public comprehensive university)

The influential segment of the liberal arts people won't give the education faculty—including me—the time of day. [Interviewer: What's the basis for that?] They think we aren't substantive, not rigorous, which simply isn't so. Except, as I said, we have had some slippage, and there has been a lot of basket weaving around here, which is unfortunate. (Professor, private comprehensive university)

An influential segment says we're dummies—that the students we produce are dummies. We do 20 percent of the students' education. They have them for 80 percent, and say we're the dummies. (Professor, private comprehensive university)

Some faculty members in arts and sciences indeed hold the view that education is not as rigorous as arts and sciences, and that education is not as useful as arts and sciences:

Teacher education is an accessory, and not central to our purpose. A good teacher can figure out how to teach. I'll bet the good teachers you [the interviewer] had never spent any time on their education courses. (Instructor, arts and sciences, private liberal arts college)

The teacher ed program is not highly regarded in A&S. Too much Mickey Mouse; no rigor. (Associate Professor, arts and sciences, public doctorate granting university)

The academic departments really think they are more elite, tougher, better. (Professor, arts and sciences, private liberal arts college)

In addition to the issue of academic rigor and usefulness of education, another frequently mentioned reason is that the university and its faculty have misplaced their priorities. In other words, the school of education and its functions have been neglected and have low priority:

We don't pay much attention to education in general, so we don't pay much attention to educating teachers. People in the disciplines do not place a high value on their responsibilities for educating teachers. The focus is on preparation of researchers in the disciplines, not on the literate scientist. (Professor, public research university)

The most prestige is accorded those who are developing esoteric theories of criticism of minor poets, while far less prestige is accorded people like me who want to develop better ways of teaching people. (Assistant Professor, public comprehensive university)

My colleagues in chemistry won't have anything to do with chemistry education. They think the education students are second class citizens. (Professor, private comprehensive university)

Related to the issue of priority is that of resource and support. Education faculty members feel that the school of education does not have enough resource and support from the university:

Education is taking a backseat to business because of the business dean who pushes business programs effectively. Salaries are different, too. The other deans are no match for the business college dean. (Associate Professor, public comprehensive university)

The A&S people get all the money; they get all the support from the administration, and spend all of their time on politics—time they should be spending on preparing for their classes, and that's why their classes are so poor. I know for a fact that their teaching is poor. I hear that from both faculty and students. The A&S people want to make this into another [high prestige liberal arts college]. (Associate Professor, public comprehensive university)

We didn't get our share of resources or staff when times were tough. But we didn't have a lot of students. Now we have a lot more students and we're hiring more staff. On the other hand, they're taking a

> classroom from us, giving it to [another department]. (Professor, public comprehensive university)

> Business gets tremendous support from the community, and support from the university. (Professor, public doctorate granting university)

The final explanation for the low status of education is the misunderstanding and miscommunication between faculties of education on one hand and arts and sciences on the other:

> Education has low status and prestige here. Our colleagues in arts and sciences don't understand what we do, but everybody across campus will be judging you as a young faculty member. (Professor, private research/doctorate granting university)

> I often wonder what they are doing over there. (Professor, arts and sciences, private liberal arts college)

> There's lots of "you guys over there," a feeling that an education major doesn't have to do anything. (Professor, public research university)

The qualitative interview data also reveal that the school of education, in general, and teacher education, in particular, have low status in academia. The reasons for the low status include the following: (a) the school of education is less rigorous than arts and sciences, (b) the university neglects the school of education and its functions by misplacing its priority, and (c) there is miscommunication between the faculties of education on one hand and arts and sciences on the other. Education faculty members appear to be resentful of the low status of, and the ever diminishing resources for, the school of education. There appears to be a vicious cycle as to the low status of, and decreasing support for, the school of education—the lower the status the school of education has, the less support it has; the fewer resources for the school of education, the even lower status it has. How does the school of education get into such a situation? We will discuss this question in the following section.

Reclaiming the Identity of the School of Education

The low status of the school of education and its faculty arises largely from its ambiguous identity. It has been torn between the academic and the professional model. The low status of the faculty and programs are related to the fact that the school of education is essentially a professional school, but it does not strongly claim so. Instead it tries to emulate what the faculty members in arts and sciences do. Then, why doesn't the school of education claim itself as a professional school as the schools of law and medicine do?

The professional schools of law and medicine enjoy higher status not only in the university but also in society at large. This is because these two professions have the following characteristics (Soder, 1989b). First, they both have a clearly defined body of technical knowledge. It takes years to become familiar with the knowledge base and the terminology of the legal and medical professions. However, a knowledge-based argument for the professional status of teaching was made only about a decade ago (Grossman, 1990; Shulman, 1987), and the knowledge base of teaching is still in its infancy. Second, the alumni of law and medical schools tend to be males who are affluent and influential in social, cultural, and political activities, while the alumni of schools of education enter a profession that is historically feminized and accorded little respect. Third, the status of a profession tends to be positively associated with that of the clients whom the profession serves. The clients of law and medicine are more powerful than those of teaching because the clients of teaching are often minors and are compelled to come to school by force of law.

Given the fact that the school of education does not have those characteristics that are enjoyed by the high-status schools of law and medicine, the school of education appears to emulate the faculty of arts and sciences (Clifford & Guthrie, 1988). As early as the turn of the century, William Payne was arguing that education is a part of the arts and sciences. Generally speaking, identifying with the faculty of arts and sciences is more prevalent in elite schools of education, a fact that is usually reflected in moving away from the involvement in educational practice, employing the methodology of sciences to *study* educational issues, and implementing a reward structure geared to the nature of arts and sciences. However, modeling after the faculty of arts and sciences does not seem to elevate the status of the school of education, an observation that is supported by both quantitative survey data and qualitative interview data.

Therefore, the school of education has been facing a lose-lose situation. On one hand, it does not have the characteristics of the schools of law and medicine. Therefore, it does not strongly and proudly claim itself to be a professional school for fear that the school of education would be at the bottom of the pecking order and called a "trade school." On the other hand, the faculty of arts and sciences will not accept the faculty of education as their peers because of the practice-oriented nature of the school of education. Soder (1989b, p. 30) summarized the dilemma of the school of education in the following:

> Early on, then, SCDEs [schools, colleges, and departments of education] got into a muddle. If viewed as professional schools, SCDEs were liable to the disadvantages of the ambivalent and contingent status of professional schools, without any of the advantages that enabled medical and law schools to maintain semi-autonomous and usually power places at or near the top of the university hierarchy. But if viewed as academic departments, in effect, in arts and sciences, then SCDEs were liable to the disadvantages of being judged by criteria having little real relevance to their actual enterprise.

Soder went on to argue that the issue of the identity of the school of education continues to face the education faculty:

> Recent reports suggest that SCDEs have done little to resolve the identity muddle. It seems that SCDEs are continuing to follow a strategy of acceding to external requirements to perform as a professional school, while simultaneously asking to have that performance judged by arts and sciences. In the past, that strategy led to just-get-on-with-it impatience on the part of university administrators, a good bit of snickering and raised eyebrows on the part of arts and sciences faculty members, and schizophrenic confusion on the part of the SCDEs. There is nothing to suggest that current efforts to emulate arts and sciences or to become big-name research institutes will lead to anything but more of the same.

There have been some discussions in recent years on the nature of the school of education. Pratte and Rury (1991, p. 59) argued that "teachers belong to a distinctive group of craft professions, quite different from the more elite expert professions commonly identified with professional status." Therefore, what Pratte and Rury suggested is that the school of education should claim its identify as a craft-oriented professional school. The third report of the Holmes Group (1995), *Tomorrow's Schools of Education*, argued along the same line, although it did not use Pratte and Rury's term. The report recommended that tomorrow's schools of education target the educational practice in lower schools. However, because the school of education has covered such a large and ambiguous territory, the call for focusing the mission of the school of education by the Holmes Group has been criticized by scholars within the school of education (e.g., Labaree & Pallas, 1996a, 1996b).

As early as 1904, John Dewey (1904) perceived that the norms of arts and sciences prevailed in then normal schools. He suggested that the school of education should claim unequivocally that it is a professional school, and that it should emulate how engineers, doctors, lawyers, and architects are educated. It appears that we have not heeded Dewey's admonition made almost a century ago, and that there is a long journey ahead of us to reclaim the identity of the school of education after a long period of ambiguity and confusion.

CHAPTER FOUR

Dimensions of Education Faculty Members' Work and Promotion Criteria

In educational practice and research, there is an assumption that the latent structure underlying faculty members' mission involvement and reward structure is invariant. In everyday conversation pertaining to higher education, we tend to use a single framework to describe the work of faculty members in all types of institutions. For example, the theory of the holy trinity—teaching, research, and service—prevails in order to conceptualize faculty members' mission involvement. When the theory of the holy trinity does not seem to capture the essence of the faculty's mission involvement, new typologies are proposed. For instance, Boyer (1990) proposes a quadruple theory of scholarship that includes discovery, integration, application, and teaching, a theory which is criticized as being applicable only to those elite research universities (Applbaum, 1993). The assumption underlying Applbaum's criticism is that other typologies might better represent faculty's work for those faculty in institutions other than elite research universities. In educational administration, the invariant framework becomes a vehicle to describe and evaluate faculty members' work (e.g., Aleamoni, 1980; Mancing, 1991; McLean, 1987; Wisniewski, 1989).

The assumption of invariance in the latent structure of faculty members' mission involvement is also evident in empirical studies (e.g., Fairweather, 1993a, 1993b; Gideonse, 1989). When Gideonse (1989) inquired into how faculty members allocated their time by asking them to keep logs of their activities for a seven-day week, the data categories were as follows:

1. Preparation for class
2. Scheduled class instruction
3. Evaluation of student performance
4. Doctoral instruction
5. Supervision of practica
6. Travel associated with supervision of practica or class instruction off-campus
7. Research and scholarship
8. Governance, including service on committees
9. Public service associated with professional associations
10. Public service associated with schools
11. Other public services such as community agencies and governmental bodies
12. Student advising (with the exception of doctoral instruction)
13. Administrative duties
14. Ceremonial responsibilities

These 14 categories were then aggregated into five composite factors: instruction, scholarship, advising, service, and administration/governance. The results were subsequently reported on these factors in relation to three institutions: College A (a private doctorate granting institution), College B (a public doctorate granting institution), and College C (a private master's degree granting institution). Gideonse's analysis assumed that the five-factor structure —instruction, scholarship, advising, service, and administration/governance—applies to the three types of colleges with equal or comparable validity.

Another example would be Fairweather's (1993a, 1993b) study on determinants of faculty salary. Corresponding to his conceptualization of the study, he collected data on 16 variables that cover both demographic and professional aspects. In order to facilitate the regression analysis, he conducted a principal components analysis to collapse age, time in rank, and years at the current institution into the first composite—"seniority," and to combine percentage of time spent on teaching and percentage of time spent on research into the second composite—"more research/less teaching." Among others, Fairweather found a similar structure of salary determinants across research universities, doctorate granting universities, comprehensive universities, and liberal arts colleges—a phenomenon he called "a single reward structure" or "homogenization of reward structure across institutional types and disciplines." Due to a large sample of about 4,000 cases, Fairweather was able to conduct a principal components analysis to collapse the variables, a process which is much more sophisticated than Gideonse's approach. However, since the principal components analysis was conducted on the whole sample rather than the sub-samples, which include research universities, doctorate granting universities, comprehensive universities, and liberal arts colleges, the question still remains whether the factor structure arising from the whole sample has equal validity for sub-samples. Many other empirical studies (e.g., Katz, 1973; Tuckman, 1976) took the same approach as Fairweather's. It seems to be a common practice in educational research to report results by employing a single set of factors, with the assumption that a single factor structure applies to all types of institutions with equal validity.

Are the Dimensions of Faculty Members' Work and Promotion Criteria the Same across Different Types of Institutions?

The latent structure of faculty members' mission involvement and promotion criteria in different types of institutions is, in and of itself, an interesting research topic. An inquiry into the latent structure of faculty members' mission involvement and promotion criteria has its theoretical and methodological implications. Theoretically, it is to test the conventional theories such as the theory of the holy trinity. Methodologically, the question of the latent structure should be inquired into before data can be aggregated for subsequent analysis. This chapter intends to inquire into whether education faculty members in three types of institutions—research universities, doctorate granting universities, and comprehensive universities as defined by the Carnegie Foundation for the Advancement of Teaching (1987)—perceive the same latent structure of mission involvement and promotion criteria by conducting principal components analyses of the data collected in the Study of Education of Educators (SEE).

Among others, the faculty survey questionnaire asked respondents to answer questions regarding missions of the school of education. These questions regarding the nine missions are constructed from two different perspectives. First, the respondents were asked to rate their current involvement in the nine missions of the school of education on a Likert scale, ranging from 1 (not at all involved), to 2 (marginally involved), 3 (moderately involved), and 4 (heavily involved). Second, the respondents were asked to rate the weight placed by their institution on each of the missions of the school of education for promotion on a Likert scale, ranging from 1 (not considered), to 2 (marginally helpful), 3 (moderately helpful), and 4 (essential).

In the survey instrument with which the data for this study were collected, the nine items in current mission involvement and promotion criteria include the following:

1. Teaching
2. Research and scholarly activity
3. Development, dissemination, and demonstration (pertains to generalizable instructional materials, teaching techniques, administrative strategies, etc., likely to be of use to a wide range of practitioners)
4. Ad hoc services to schools and other educational agencies (pertains to paid and/or unpaid consultant services on an as-needed basis)
5. Effecting changes in public schools (pertains to involvement in long-term programs of educational change and school improvement)
6. Professional preparation of school teachers
7. Professional preparation of special educators, i.e., teachers of handicapped learners (learning disabled, behaviorally disordered, mentally retarded, etc.)
8. Professional preparation of school administrators
9. Preparation of researchers and/or future university/college faculty members

Table 4.1

Results of Principal Components Analyses for Research, Doctorate Granting, Comprehensive, and All Universities

	RU				DGU				CU				All			
	PC1	PC2	PC3	PC4	PC1	PC2	PC3	PC4	PC1	PC2	PC3	PC4	PC1	PC2	PC3	PC4
Current Mission Involvement																
Teaching			.78				.81				.58				.83	
Research and scholarly activity		.83				.83			.45					.84		
Development, dissemination, and demonstration	.83				.75				.81				.80			
Ad hoc services to schools and other agencies	.79				.82				.82				.82			
Effecting changes in public schools	.77				.82				.73				.79			
Preparation of school teachers			.78				.74				.79				.75	
Preparation of special educators				.75				.70		.71						.76
Preparation of school administrators				.70				.78		.72						.72
Preparation of researchers and/or college faculty		.78				.83				.70				.81		
Percent of variance accounted for after rotation	22	17	15	14	23	17	16	14	24	19	15		23	17	15	14
Current Promotion Criteria																
Teaching		.70									-.79				-.56	
Research and scholarly activity			.93				.76				.63				.73	
Development, dissemination, and demonstration		.75				.79				.77				.81		
Ad hoc services to schools and other agencies		.73				.81				.82				.80		
Effecting changes in public schools	.52	.57				.74				.69				.69		
Preparation of school teachers	.70	.49			.88				.78				.79			
Preparation of special educators	.84				.92				.84				.86			
Preparation of school administrators	.85				.90				.83				.87			
Preparation of researchers and/or college faculty	.70					.74			.50		.53		.41		.74	
Percent of variance accounted for after rotation	31	25	12		31	22	15		27	23	16		29	24	16	

Due to the nature of the existing database, such aspects as administration and committee work are not included in the analysis. Nonetheless, these nine items represent major aspects of education faculty members' work. In addition, the purpose of the study is to illustrate the variance of the latent structure of mission involvement and promotion criteria rather than to arrive at a definitive latent structure.

Principal components analyses were conducted by using SPSS on the VAX mainframe. As a rule of thumb, it is comforting to have at least five cases for each observed variable when principal components analysis is conducted (Tabachnick & Fidell, 1989, p. 603). For this analysis, there are nine observed variables in each set; therefore, a sample size of 45 is required for conducting principal components analysis. The sample sizes for research, doctorate granting, and comprehensive universities are 312, 290, and 316, respectively. Therefore, the data are adequate for conducting reliable principal components analysis.

For all of the following analyses, principal components extraction with pairwise deletion and varimax rotation was used to collapse nine observed variables into principal components. Varimax rotation was employed because of its conceptual simplicity and ease of description. In accordance with the suggestions in statistical textbooks (e.g., Kachigan, 1991; Stevens, 1992), principal components with eigenvalues greater than 1.0 were retained, rotated, and reported in Table 4.1; loadings less than .39 are not displayed in Table 4.1 because a coefficient less than .39 accounts for less than 15% of the variance and displaying loadings less than .39 would complicate the latent structures.

The results of the principal components analysis of current mission involvement and promotion criteria are displayed in Table 4.1. Faculty members in research and doctorate granting universities appear to have the same latent structure of current mission involvement, which includes four principal components: (a) service, (b) research and preparation of researchers, (c) teaching and preparation of teachers, and (d) preparation of school administrators and special educators. For faculty members in comprehensive universities, there are three principal components in current mission involvement: (a) research, development, and service; (b) preparation of special educators, school administrators, and researchers; and (c) teaching and preparation of teachers. When faculty members from the three types of institutions are combined together, the result of principal components analysis is identical to that for faculty members in research and doctorate granting universities.

The analysis suggests both similarity and dissimilarity in the latent structure of current mission involvement as perceived by three faculty groups. It appears that only one factor—teaching and preparation of teachers—is consistent across the three different types of institutions. There are, however, three major differences between faculty members in research and doctorate granting universities on the one hand and those in comprehensive universities on the other. First, there are four principal components for faculty members in research and doctorate universities while there are three for those in comprehensive universities. This indicates that faculty members in research and doctorate granting universities perceive a more diversified mission than their counterparts in comprehensive universities. Second, research and preparation of researchers form a principal component for faculty members in research and doctorate granting universities, while for those in comprehensive universities, research is perceived as more associated with development and providing service to schools. It appears that the construct of research is "purer" for faculty members in research and doctorate granting universities, but more "conglomerate" for those in comprehensive universities. Finally, faculty members in research and doctorate granting universities distinguish preparation of special educators and school administrators from researchers, but faculty members in comprehensive universities lump preparation of the three kinds of personnel into one principal component. Given all these similarities and dissimilarities, principal components analyses reveal that there is no consistent latent structure in current mission involvement across the three types of institutions. This finding is contrary to the holy trinity theory of teaching, research, and service, a theory which presumably applies to all types of institutions. There are elements of teaching, research, and service in education faculty's work, but they do not necessarily perceive their work in the framework of the traditional tripartite responsibility.

The principal components analysis on current promotion criteria as perceived by faculty members in the research university, doctorate granting university, comprehensive university, and all three kinds of institutions combined (Table 4.1), reveals four different sets of the latent structure. Again the results are not consistent with the assumption of invariance of the latent structure across institutional types. Among many interesting observations that could be drawn from the analyses on current promotion criteria, this author wants to focus on the following two. First, for faculty members in research universities, "research and scholarly activity" alone constitutes a principal component with loading as high as .93, an indication that research is a distinctive dimension for faculty promotion in research universities. Second, for faculty members in the three types of institutions, separate or combined, the preparation of school teachers, special educators, and school administrators are associated. So are development, ad hoc services to schools, and effecting changes in schools. This suggests that the elements of preparation of school educators and service are consistent across institutional types, although these two elements alone or together with other variables constitute different principal components across institutional types.

Inconsistency is not just found across institutional types as to the latent structure of current mission involvement and promotion criteria. Even within a certain type, there is variation in the latent structure across current mission involvement and current promotion criteria. It appears that for faculty members in all three types of institutions, separate or combined, the latent structure of current mission involvement is not consistent with that of current promotion criteria, a discrepancy that might have contributed to the tension between what faculty members are doing and how they are rewarded, as it is revealed in many studies (e.g., AACTE, 1987, 1988, 1990, 1992; Carnegie Foundation, 1989; Moses, 1986; Soder, 1990b).

Policy Implications

Varying latent structures within and across institutional types question the assumption of the invariance of the latent structure in mission involvement and promotion criteria. The analyses of this study suggest that there should be multiple theories or frameworks to conceptualize, describe, and evaluate faculty members' work. The data for this analysis are confined to faculty members in research, doctorate granting, and comprehensive universities. When faculty members from liberal arts and community colleges are taken into account, the variance of the latent structure might be further illustrated. Lack of a consistent latent structure within each type of institution also points out the mismatch between mission involvement and promotion criteria, a concern that has been addressed in educational research and practice.

The findings of this study also have methodological implications for research. As mentioned in the introduction, Gideonse (1989) collapsed 14 categories into five factors and then aggregated data on these five factors for three different kinds of institutions. In light of the findings in this chapter, Gideonse's method of aggregating data is questionable because these factors do not necessarily have the same meaning for faculty members in different types of institutions. In other words, it is inappropriate to assume that concepts such as instruction, scholarship, and service have the same construct validity in different types of institutions. The same criticism can be extended to Fairweather's study because his principal components analysis on the whole sample rather than sub-samples has the same assumptions as Gideonse's.

The analysis presented in the foregoing has its limitations. First, it is a fact that the principal components analyses inquire only into some major aspects of education faculty members' work. Some other aspects, such as administration and committee work, are not included. However, this author doubts there would be a single latent structure emerging for all types of institutions across current mission involvement and promotion criteria if other aspects of education faculty's work were included. The nature of the findings will remain unchanged even if more variables are included. Second, the analysis only inquired into education faculty members' mission involvement and promotion criteria. Education faculty members, differing from arts and sciences faculty as well as faculty in professional schools as represented by the business school and the law school (Clifford & Guthrie, 1988; Goodlad, 1990b), have their own unique characteristics. More research should be conducted on faculty members of arts and sciences and other professional schools. However, further inquires are more likely to support the thesis of this chapter and argue against the assumption of the invariance of the latent structure across institutional types and disciplines. The analysis in this chapter is just one of the first steps to improve our understanding of the latent structure of faculty members' mission involvement and promotion criteria.

CHAPTER FIVE

Mission Involvement and Promotion Criteria

Education Faculty Members' Mission Involvement

Within the context of diversification of education faculty members' mission, how they allocate time becomes an interesting research topic. The 1988 RATE study (AACTE, 1988) surveyed 153 secondary methods faculty members, probing into how education professors in three types of institutions—those that granted bachelor's, master's, and doctoral degrees—allocated their time to advising, teaching, research, administration, preparation, and community service. It was found that the major areas of faculty effort were evenly divided among the three types of institutions, except in administration and research. Faculty members in doctorate granting institutions spent more than twice as much time on research (10.7 hours per week) than faculty members in bachelor's degree granting institutions (3.6 hours per week) and master's degree granting institutions (4.2 hours per week). Faculty members in bachelor's degree granting institutions allocated considerably more time to administration (11.7 hours per week) than faculty members in master's degree granting institutions (6.7 hours per week) and doctorate granting institutions (3.2 hours per week).

The 1992 RATE study had 316 respondents from 65 schools of education. These respondents spent, on the average, 48 hours per week on professional activities. The distribution of hours on different activities was as follows: advising, 5.3; class preparation, 11.7; undergraduate teaching, 7.7; graduate teaching, 3.3; in-service, 1.5; research/scholarly work, 6.9; committee work, 3.7; administrative tasks, 4.9; and other, 3.5. It is apparent that most of the time was spent on teaching-related activities. There was again some variation among the faculty members in different types of institutions. Faculty members in bachelor's degree granting institutions reported spending relatively more time preparing for class and teaching undergraduates compared to faculty members in master's degree and doctorate granting institutions, where more time was allocated to research. Committee work and administrative tasks consumed more time in master's degree and doctorate granting institutions (AACTE, 1992).

Gideonse (1989) inquired into how 27 faculty members allocated their time by asking them to keep logs of their activities for a seven-day week, recording the amount of time they spent on instruction, scholarship, advising, service, and administration/governance. The results were then reported on these composite categories in relation to three institutions: College A (a private, doctorate granting institution), College B (a public, doctorate granting institution), and College C (a private, master's degree granting institution).

Gideonse reported that there was some variation within each college on each of the five composite categories. The most dramatic difference appeared in the area of research, ranging from zero to 35.5 hours per week for individual faculty members. Gideonse's data and analysis also supported the generalization that those who devote their energies to instruction spend less time on scholarship. The between-college analysis suggested that faculty members in doctorate granting institutions (College A and College B) spent more time on scholarship, 28.6 and 17.3 hours respectively, but less on instruction, 37.3 and 34.7 hours respectively, than faculty members in the master's degree granting institution (College C), where faculty allocated 6.8 and 51 hours to research and instruction, respectively.

In addition to inquiry into time allocation patterns of education faculty members, another perspective on their mission involvement is to study the relationship between what education faculty members are doing, what they are expected to do, and what they desire to do. Two of five RATE studies inquired into actual, expected, and ideal allocation of time for education faculty. The 1987 RATE study of 215 secondary methods faculty reported that education faculty wanted to reduce their actual time on teaching from 60% to 53%, but to increase their time on research from 15% to 22%, and on service from 22% to 27% (AACTE, 1987).

The 1990 RATE study of 251 faculty members in elementary education suggested a similar pattern (AACTE, 1990). Across all three types of institutions, faculty members desired to reduce their time on teaching (from about 65% to 55%) while increasing time on research, with faculty members in master's degree and doctorate granting institutions hoping to double their time on research (from 13% to 25%). As to the time for service, faculty members in doctorate granting institutions desired to increase slightly while faculty members in master's degree and bachelor's degree granting institutions wanted to decrease slightly. The 1992 RATE study (AACTE, 1992) of 316 education faculty members and Soder's (1989a) inquiry into 1,217 education faculty members suggested a pattern similar to those suggested by the 1987 and 1990 RATE studies (AACTE, 1987, 1990).

A few interesting observations emerge from the review of the studies of education faculty members' time allocation. First, institutional type is a mediate factor in analyzing data and reporting research findings, and there seems to be some variation among types of institutions in education faculty members' involvement in various missions. However, as Gideonse reported in his study, there is considerable variation within institutional type as well. Second, it is a common practice to report results by employing the same set of categories, with the assumption that these categories apply to all types of institutions with equal validity. Gideonse collapsed 14 categories into five composite categories without asking whether faculty members in the three types of institutions have the same factor structure of involvement in those 14 categories. The factor structure of education faculty members' involvement in education missions in different types of institution is, in and of itself, an interesting topic. Strictly speaking, the question of the latent structure should be inquired into before data are aggregated for subsequent analysis. Third, there is a discrepancy between what education faculty members are doing, what they are expected to do by their institutions, and what they wish they were doing. Faculty members across institutional types would prefer to decrease their time allocated to teaching and administrative duties while increasing time allocated to research, a trend that implies the nature of the reward structure on campus.

Other Factors Influencing Mission Involvement

In addition to institutional types, other factors are associated with faculty members' mission involvement. Zey-Ferrell and Ervin's study (1985) suggested that peers, chairpersons, and deans affected, in different ways, faculty members' work. Overwhelmingly, peers had the strongest effect, followed by chairpersons and deans.

Neumann and Finaly-Neumann's inquiry (1990) revealed that discipline and faculty career stage influenced faculty's commitment to their university. Their analysis suggested that faculty commitment to their university differed across disciplines. They studied faculty members in education, electrical engineering, physics, and sociology and found that faculty members in applied fields (education and electrical engineering) demonstrated a stronger commitment to their university than their counterparts in pure fields (physics and sociology). Neumann and Finaly-Neumann speculated that the difference might be due to the fact that faculty members in applied disciplines made a deliberate choice to become faculty members, while faculty members in pure disciplines might not have made such a choice.

Another factor that distinguishes faculty commitment is career stage. Neumann and Finaly-Neumann's (1990) analysis showed that university commitment reached its maximal point among senior faculty members, whereas no significant differences were found between faculty members in pre-tenure stage and mid-career stage.

In summary, the existing literature suggests that there are three major factors influencing faculty members' mission involvement—institutional factors, disciplinary factors such as pure versus applied disciplines or fields, and individual factors such as career stage.

The Relation between Work and Reward Structure

Faculty members' work and their reward structure have been frequently visited topics in the literature. The traditional tripartite role of being a faculty member—teaching, research, and service—has been under scrutiny recently, and the public's trust in higher education is eroding (Fairweather 1992, 1993a, 1993c, 1996). The Study Group on the Conditions of Excellence in American Higher Education (Study Group, 1984) recommends that investment in undergraduate education is crucial in regaining the public trust. Boyer (1986, 1987) and Bok (1992) make a similar recommendation, emphasizing the balance between research and teaching.

Most of the studies on mission involvement and reward structure focus on the role of teaching and research in the reward structure. Research-related activities are perceived to have a very prominent role in the faculty reward structure (e.g., Bok, 1991; Burch, 1989; Carnegie Foundation for the Advancement of Teaching, 1989; Clark, 1987; Lonsdale, 1993). This is the case not only in the United States, but also in other Western countries (e.g., Moses, 1987).

Involvement in research is found consistently to be positively correlated with reward, whether reward is in the form of pay, promotion, or tenure (Fairweather, 1993a, 1993b; Fulton & Trow, 1974; Katz, 1973; Rossman, 1976; Siegfried & White, 1973; Tuckman, 1976; Tuckman, Gapinski, & Hageman, 1977; Tuckman & Hagemann 1976; Tuckman & Leahy, 1975). As to the relative importance of the volume of published work as opposed to its quality, analyses indicate that the quantity of publications is far more important than the various measures of quality of publications (Long, Allison, & McGinnis, 1993). Since research is the most important predictor for faculty salary across all types of institutions as well as disciplines, Fairweather (1993b) summarizes that there is an institutional and professional homogenization in the faculty reward structure across disciplines and types of institutions.

The review of literature on the relationship between teaching and reward reveals a confusing territory (Fairweather, 1993b, p. 604):

> Teaching has been found positively related to salary and promotion (Hoyt, 1974; Kasten, 1984; Katz, 1973; Koch and Chizmar, 1973; Rossman, 1976; Salthouse, McKeachie, and Lin, 1978; Siegfried and White; 1973), unrelated to salary and promotion (Tuckman, Gapinski, and Hagemann, 1977; Tuckman and Hagemann, 1976), and negatively related to salary and promotion (Marsh and Dillon, 1980).

Fairweather's (1993a, 1993b) studies on more than 4,000 full-time, tenure-track faculty members in four-year colleges and universities suggest that teaching activities are seldom rewarded; in some cases, time spent on teaching is negatively related to salary. In other words, involvement in teaching is at best a neutral factor in predicting salary and at worst a negative predictor of pay. Although the relationship between teaching and reward is inconclusive and ambiguous, suffice it to point out that the patterns of the relationship found in the studies on teaching and reward are dramatically different from the consistently positive relationship found between research and reward.

Studies inquiring into the role of service and administration in reward structure indicate that public service yields low compensation (Tuckman et al., 1977), or that public service is not related or negatively related to salary (Fairweather, 1993a, 1993b). Involvement in administration, on the other hand, is found to be positively related to salary (Fairweather, 1993a, 1993b; Tuckman et al., 1977).

The paramount importance of research in the faculty members' reward structure is also evident in research on the education faculty's reward structure. Many of the teacher preparation institutions evolved from normal schools to teachers' colleges to state colleges and to regional state universities. This transition, virtually completed by the early 1970s, was accompanied by a severe loss of identity by teacher education (Goodlad, 1990a; Howey & Zimpher, 1989, 1990). Teacher education, once the only mission of these institutions, is now just *one* of the many businesses in the multi-purpose institutions (Kerr, 1994; National Institute of Education, 1985).

Along with the evolution of many teacher education institutions is the increasing importance of research in the reward system for education faculty members (e.g., Ducharme, 1993; Ducharme & Agne, 1986; Ducharme & Kluender, 1990; Goodlad, 1990a; Lawson, 1990). Based on interviews in 29 colleges and universities, Soder (1989a, 1989b, 1990b) found that a shift from teaching to research is present in all schools of education, although there is variance among flagship public, major public, regional public, major private, regional private, and liberal arts institutions, with flagship public and major private universities at one end of the continuum and liberal arts colleges at the other.

Through research we know some aspects of mission involvement and reward structure of higher education faculty members, in general, and education faculty members, in particular. The analysis in this chapter intends to contribute to our knowledge on this topic by studying the relationship between education faculty members' mission involvement and promotion criteria. The analysis in this chapter differs from previous studies in the following two aspects.

The analysis inquires into various aspects of mission involvement (see below) and promotion criteria, and the relationship between mission involvement and promotion criteria. Most past studies used salary as the criterion measure, a variable that cannot be articulated in terms of the various possible missions of the school of education. By inquiring into how education faculty members are involved in the nine missions as defined in the following, and how these nine missions are important for promotion purposes, this study is able to reveal a dynamic picture regarding the relationship between mission involvement and promotion criteria.

The purpose of the analysis in this chapter is to examine the relationship between faculty members' involvement in an articulated set of missions of the school of education, on the one hand, and the extent to which these missions are used as promotion criteria, on the other. Furthermore, this study will inquire into whether the relationship changes depending on institutional type. The findings and conclusions will provide part of the knowledge base for dealing with the problems of faculty morale and institutional health. Although 49% of the faculty chose "very good place" when they were asked "In general, how do you feel about your institution?" the percentages were lower for faculty members in four-year institutions than for those in two-year ones. The percentages were as low as 37% and 39% for faculty members in doctorate granting and comprehensive universities, respectively (Carnegie Foundation for the Advancement of Teaching, 1989, p. 95). Soder's (1990b) surveys of, and in-depth interviews with, faculty members in education reveal that considerable unhappiness exists among many faculty members about their institutional work and that there are considerable gaps between what they say they want to do and what they say their institutions require them to do. Older faculty members feel that they are being pushed aside with the change of reward structure, while younger ones feel the pressure of "publish or perish." There seems to be a discrepancy between faculty members' perceptions of their work (what I am calling "mission involvement") and the reward structure by which their work is evaluated.

Background of the Survey

In this chapter, education faculty members were defined as tenure-line faculty members associated with the school of education (please refer to the appendix for a detailed description of the sample). After excluding the respondents not on a tenure-line, valid cases for research, doctorate granting, and comprehensive universities were 312, 290, and 316, respectively. Since there were only 30 respondents from the four liberal arts colleges, analyses could not be reliably conducted on faculty members in those institutions. Therefore, liberal arts colleges were not included in the current study. In sum, the data source for this study included 918 tenure-line faculty members in 25 institutions: 312 faculty members in 8 research universities, 290 faculty members in 6 doctorate granting universities, and 316 faculty members in 11 comprehensive universities.

The faculty survey questionnaire asked respondents to answer questions regarding missions of the school of education from three different perspectives. First, respondents were asked to rate their current involvement in the nine missions of the school of education on a Likert scale, ranging from 1 (not at all involved), to 2 (marginally involved), 3 (moderately involved), and 4 (heavily involved). Second, the respondents were asked to rate the weight placed by their institution on each of the nine missions of the school of education for promotion on a Likert scale, ranging from 1 (not considered), to 2 (marginally helpful), 3 (moderately helpful), and 4 (essential). Finally, respondents were asked to indicate, by using the same scale they used on their responses to the current promotion criteria, the desired weight for promotion that should be placed on each of the missions.

Factor analyses were conducted to inquire into whether the nine items could be collapsed so as to simplify the following analyses. The results of factor analyses indicated that there was no consistent latent structure across current mission involvement and current and desired promotion criteria for each type of institution, and that there was no consistent latent structure across all three institutional types in current mission involvement, current promotion criteria, and desired promotion criteria.

Although some other aspects, such as administration and committee work, were not included in the nine items, this author doubts that there would be a single latent structure emerging for all types of institutions across current mission involvement and current and desired promotion criteria if other aspects of faculty's work were included. Since there is no single latent structure across the three types of institutions and across current mission involvement and current and desired promotion criteria, it is impossible to employ a single scheme to collapse the nine items for subsequent analyses. Although it is an acceptable practice to drop some items and then focus on such major items as teaching, research, and preparation of school teachers, this author chooses to keep all nine missions in the ensuing analyses so as to reveal a more comprehensive picture regarding education faculty members' mission involvement and promotion criteria.

The approach for data analysis here is to inquire into faculty members' average involvement in the missions of the school of education and the average weight of each mission in current and desired promotion criteria. Rank order is then assigned on the basis of the mean, and rank-order correlation is calculated to inquire into the congruence or discrepancy between mission involvement and promotion criteria. In the first approach, each mission's weight in current and desired promotion criteria is calculated without taking into account faculty members' level of involvement, a moderating variable that is incorporated into the second approach. The purpose of the second approach is to inquire into the issues of the common core and unity or diversity of promotion criteria. If both the high- and low-involvement groups in a certain mission perceive that this mission has a very heavy weight in promotion criteria, the mission seems to be the common core of promotion criteria. If the high- and low-involvement groups of a certain mission perceive significantly different weights of this mission in promotion criteria, the mission seems to have diversified weights for faculty members with different levels of involvement.

The Dominance of Research in the Promotion Criteria
as Reflected in the Quantitative Survey Data

Mean and rank of how faculty members in research, doctorate granting, and comprehensive universities perceive current mission involvement, current promotion criteria, and desired promotion criteria are reported in Table 5.1. Based on the rank in Table 5.1, Spearman's rank-order correlation between current mission involvement and current and desired promotion criteria is conducted and displayed in Table 5.2.

The rank-order correlation analyses indicate that for all three faculty groups, rank-order correlation between current mission involvement and desired promotion criteria (.92, .92, and .88 for faculty members in research, doctorate granting, and comprehensive universities, respectively) is greater than that between current mission involvement and current promotion criteria (.82, .52, and .70 for faculty members in research, doctorate granting, and comprehensive universities, respectively). This suggests that education faculty members desire that the promotion criteria should be more compatible with their current mission involvement. Faculty members in doctorate granting universities particularly feel that there is a discrepancy between their current mission involvement and current promotion criteria ($rs = .52, p > .05$).

The rank-order correlation based on all nine items might conceal some of the patterns in relation to particular items. For example, faculty members perceive that they are currently most involved in teaching, with their involvement in research ranging from the second to the fifth rank, depending on institutional type. However, the ranks of teaching and research are reversed when current promotion criteria are concerned. Research has the first rank in current promotion criteria while teaching has second place for all faculty groups. When desired promotion criteria are concerned, the ranks of teaching and research are reversed again from those in current promotion criteria, with the notable exception of faculty members in comprehensive universities, for whom preparation of teachers moves to second priority followed by research in third place. A closer inquiry into teaching and research reveals the discrepancy between current mission involvement and current promotion criteria as well as the desire to

Table 5.1

Means and Ranks of Faculty Members' Perceptions of Current Mission Involvement, Current Promotion Criteria, and Desired Promotion Criteria

Items	Current mission involvement		Current promotion criteria		Desired promotion criteria	
	Mean	Rank	Mean	Rank	Mean	Rank
			Research universities			
Teaching	3.54	1	2.82	2	3.75	1
Research and scholarly activity	3.19	2	3.88	1	3.59	2
Development, dissemination, and demonstration	2.50	5	2.29	4	2.85	6
Ad hoc services to schools	2.46	7	1.95	8	2.63	9
Effecting change in public schools	2.47	6	1.76	9	2.89	5
Preparation of school teachers	2.81	4	2.24	5	3.24	3
Preparation of special educators	1.80	9	2.11	7	2.64	8
Preparation of school administrators	1.88	8	2.14	6	2.69	7
Preparation of researchers and/or university faculty	2.91	3	2.80	3	3.23	4
			Doctorate granting universities			
Teaching	3.65	1	3.27	2	3.80	1
Research and scholarly activity	2.84	3	3.64	1	3.29	2
Development, dissemination, and demonstration	2.53	5	2.49	6	2.80	5
Ad hoc services to schools	2.65	4	2.38	7	2.83	4
Effecting change in public schools	2.41	7	1.88	9	2.73	7
Preparation of school teachers	3.09	2	2.63	3	3.24	3
Preparation of special educators	1.94	8	2.51	5	2.76	6
Preparation of school administrators	1.79	9	2.52	4	2.68	9
Preparation of researchers and/or university faculty	2.48	6	2.37	8	2.72	8
			Comprehensive universities			
Teaching	3.76	1	3.43	2	3.86	1
Research and scholarly activity	2.59	5	3.50	1	3.12	3
Development, dissemination, and demonstration	2.65	3	2.68	4	2.96	4
Ad hoc services to schools	2.60	4	2.55	6	2.85	6.5
Effecting change in public schools	2.53	6	2.05	8	2.86	5
Preparation of school teachers	3.30	2	2.84	3	3.42	2
Preparation of special educators	2.08	7	2.63	5	2.85	6.5
Preparation of school administrators	1.66	9	2.40	7	2.50	8
Preparation of researchers and/or university faculty	1.80	8	1.93	9	2.25	9

Table 5.2

Rank-Order Correlation between Current Involvement and Current and Desired Promotion Criteria in the Research, Doctorate Granting, and Comprehensive University

	RU	DGU	CU
Current mission involvement and current promotion criteria	.82**	.52	.70*
Current mission involvement and desired promotion criteria	.92**	.92**	.88**

*p < .05; **p < .01.

make the promotion criteria more compatible with mission involvement.

The results displayed in Table 5.1 attest to the dominance of research in current promotion criteria, a phenomenon that is widely reported in the literature. Research is perceived to have the highest weight in current promotion criteria by faculty members in all three types of institutions despite historical differences between the several institutional types and their ostensible institutional missions. The pressure to publish as documented in the literature is supported by the data of this study. In comparison to research, it is disquieting to notice that effecting changes in schools and providing ad hoc services to public schools have very low weights in current promotion criteria. Even the preparation of school teachers, once the only mission for those institutions evolved from normal schools, has only a moderate weight in current promotion criteria.

However, faculty members—whether they are in research, doctorate granting, or comprehensive universities—desire that the prominent role of research in current promotion criteria be lowered and that weights for all the other missions in the promotion criteria be raised. As a matter of fact, research is the only item for which there is a consistent decrease in weight from current to desired promotion criteria, while for all the other eight items, there is an increase in weight. The tension between research and other missions of the school of education in making promotion decisions is evident.

The Dominance of Research in Promotion Criteria
as Reflected in Qualitative Interview Data

The interview data obtained from faculty members indicate an emphasis on research in the promotion criteria, a phenomenon that is present in almost all types of higher education institutions:

> Research and writing is the only way you get promoted, but it's not enough to write for the field—you have to write for your colleagues. We had a man in math ed who didn't get promoted because he just published in teacher education magazines. The staff dwindled when enrollment dropped in the 70s. Largely research people hired in the 80s—they haven't been in teacher education. (Male, Professor of English Education in a public research university, 26 years)

> Absolutely publish. I don't think it's changed. Other people will say that it has. They were told, they say, that teaching and service were equally important, but I don't think so. Teaching is not even an evaluation category. (Female, Associate Professor of Curriculum and Instruction in a public doctorate granting university, 18 years)

> Now it's publishing. Until 4–5 years ago, it wasn't publishing. It was teaching and committee assignments, it was an automatic promotion. Now, you can get an infinite number of points for publishing, but a finite number of points for presentations and everything else. (Male, Associate Professor of Research and Psychology at a public comprehensive university, 12 years)

> Publish, that's the main thing. We also talk about service and teaching, but from a practical point of view, they don't count very much. You know, our dean is a [he snorts] scholar. His view of scholarship is to go into a musty old library, digging up stuff about an old writer who nobody reads or cares about and then writing a book that nobody will read anyway, that's his view of scholarship. (Male, Professor of Educational Administration in a private research/doctorate granting university, 18 years)

> The reward structure is the same as everywhere, it seems. A lot of publishing is now expected, a change in the last five years. We've lost a lot of good people who came in here to teach and didn't get tenure. The administration wants to go *national*, believe it or not.

They're already regional, they think, and are positioning themselves for bigger and better things. (Associate Professor of Counseling in a private comprehensive university, 6 years)

Even in regional public universities, a place where teaching used to dominate the reward structure, some faculty members suggested that the weight of teaching in promotion criteria is quite limited:

Above all else, first, publication and scholarly work, then politics, which are incredibly important, as are personalities; third, it's necessary to be here quite a few years, and then there's social grace. Teaching and service will not have an impact on promotion, unless you are *really* crummy. Good teaching and service will be, at best, non-negative. (Male, Associate Professor of Elementary Education, 4 years)

You *must* be a teacher. Student evaluations are taken quite seriously. You can talk bullshit as long as it's rated high by the students. (Male, Professor of School Psychology, 12 years)

During the interviews, some faculty members, particularly those relatively senior faculty members, pointed out that the move from a teaching-centered reward structure to a research-dominated one has occurred in the last 20 years for flagship and major universities. However, it is a recent change for regional universities:

Now, it's generate dollars, which will translate into research where publications will accrue. Fifteen years ago, getting tenure and promotion was like high schools—letter in the mail, congratulations. Last dozen years is when the publishing and research emphasis changed. (Male, Associate Professor of Agriculture in a public research university, 6 years)

[Interviewer: "Has the reward structure changed?"] Oh *yes*, a lot. We were always expected to do some scholarly work along with everything else. But not like now. Now, they've got an idea we should have a national, even international, reputation for productivity. I don't know what's going to happen after my generation retires. They place such an emphasis on research and such a low emphasis on teaching. The young faculty come here, you can't blame them for wanting to do research and ignore teaching because they know they have to. Sooner or later it's going to catch up with us. Legislators are going to send their kids here, there will be nobody here to teach these kids, except TAs, and then you'll see funding cutbacks like never before. (Male, Professor of Science Education in a public doctorate granting university, 32 years)

It's changed. When I came in 1971, I was promoted to associate in three years. [He pauses, his face reddens; he begins to get a bit defensive.] We could go through divorces, child custody, all that, but that's just an excuse. It's stiffer competition now. People *come in* with 3, 4, 5 articles, 2, 3 grants. (Male, Associate Professor of Educational Foundations in a public doctorate granting university, 17 years)

The reward structure changed from primarily teaching in 1975. I wanted to teach. The young folks don't know anything else [other than the current reward structure]. A person like me [a slight shrug of the shoulders], I'm tolerated." (Male, Professor of Math Education in a public doctorate university, 25 years)

It's research and publishing to get tenure and associate professor. But after that, there's no reward structure here at all. You get paid basically the same whether you are doing anything or not. We have 50 people or so, total, of which about 10 are producing, doing research, publishing. "What we need now is more research, more publications," according to what I'm hearing. (Male, Professor of Science Education in a private research/doctorate granting university, 19 years)

With the increasing emphasis on research and scholarship, it becomes more and more crucial to measure research and scholarship. However, the interview data seem to indicate that research and scholarship are difficult to define, that the definitions are evolving, and that they tend to be defined quite narrowly. This is particularly true for regional universities where the move to a research-dominated reward structure was a recent development.

When I first came here, you could get tenure without any scholarly productivity or publishing. [Interviewer: "What do you mean by scholarly productivity?"] It can include a lot of things—going to professional meetings, for example. (Male, Professor of Secondary Education in a comprehensive university, 14 years)

All new faculty will be researchers as well as teachers, but you can do all sorts of publishing—convention papers, for instance, versus [a major research institution] where you'd need a book. (Male, Professor of Educational Psychology in a public comprehensive university, 12 years)

I'd say publications, that's where to put your time. You've got to do your job, though, which means teaching. In our department, as long as you do average teaching, you'll get by. You could get some service reports, working with school districts, considered as scholarly work. Maybe 2–3 articles in 7 years, and reasonable teaching. There's a pretty wide interpretation of scholarly research. It's changing slowly. In 1968, there was no publishing requirement at all, now, there's some emphasis. (Male, Professor of Educational Administration in a public comprehensive university, 20 years)

You want to know how it works in [her department]? Okay. If you get in [a leading journal] that's 4 points. [Another leading journal] is 3 points, a journal like [journal oriented to applied high school teaching] is the lowest—that gets you 1 point. If you're second author, only half the points. (Female, Professor of Speech Communication in a public comprehensive university, 18 years)

Publishing henceforth will be the name of the game. I keep a daily journal to keep track of what I'm doing. We'll be called on to do monthly reports. I keep two calendars, one in my bag here, one in the house for documentation. [The dean] said to us in no uncertain terms that the next merit increases and tenure and promotion would be based on research and publishing. When I came it was teaching, service, advisement, and creative activities. (Female, Professor of Education in a public comprehensive university, 8 years)

His view [the dean of a school of education] of scholarship is to go into a musty old library, digging up stuff about an old writer who nobody reads or cares about and then writing a book that nobody will read anyway, that's his view of scholarship. (Male, Professor of Educational Administration in a public comprehensive university, 18 years)

With research gaining more and more weight in the reward structure and research being narrowly defined, there is a debate between faculty members as to what should be rewarded:

In 1969, the rewards here were centered on being a good teacher and providing service to students. In the last several years it's changed to publication, research, scholarly work, making a contribution to one's academic field. "Pure" research is emphasized. I do lots of inservice in the districts, there's *no* reward for that. For example, I work with teachers on how to present short stories. They'll say you're just having *fun*. (Female, Professor of Speech Communication in a public comprehensive university, 18 years)

We put out a lot of reports and publications for school districts, educational service districts, really useful stuff, helping people solve the tough problems. Now, your pure research people, they'll say that kind of publication doesn't count, well I say it counts more. They say you have to have juried publications, well, we always said that we were writing for the toughest audience in the world—school boards and such. (Male, Professor of Educational Administration in a public comprehensive university, 17 years)

Most faculty think this should be a teaching institution, but that's not what the reward structure is. One professor did lots of work with an alternative school, and he did other projects with students, he didn't get promoted to full. (Male, Associate Professor of Educational Psychology in a public comprehensive university, 12 years)

Summary

Both quantitative and qualitative analyses in this chapter indicate that education faculty members perceive the current promotion criteria to be relatively uniform—research first, teaching second. However, they would like to reverse the weight of research and teaching and give higher weight to all mission activities other than research. Thus, there is a tension between what faculty members do and how they are rewarded.
      There seems to be an internal tension within the school of education between the work of individual faculty members and the institutional promotion criteria. This study found that research dominates the current promotion criteria in the institutions of the

sample, while providing services to schools and the education of educators have low weights in current mission involvement and promotion criteria. Providing services to schools and effecting changes in public schools have low weights even in the desired promotion criteria. These findings point also to an external tension between the conduct of the school of education and some expectations of society. The central issue of this external tension is the nature and function of the school of education. Both kinds of tension are worthy of further discussion in the final chapter.

CHAPTER SIX

Unity and Diversity of the Promotion Criteria

This chapter inquires into the relationship between faculty members' work and promotion criteria in the school of education. It first reviews the literature on the determinants of the reward structure. Then it discusses the changing institutional context of the school of education and the accompanying diversification of the mission and faculty, and raises the issue of how to equitably reward faculty members in institutions that have diversified missions and faculty groups. Finally, it analyzes the relationship between the education faculty's work and promotion criteria by studying quantitative survey data from a national sample of 918 tenure-line faculty members and qualitative interview data from a small sample.

Determinants of the Reward Structure

Reward structure has many aspects. In the literature, inquiry into the reward structure has been conducted from the following perspectives: salary (Fairweather, 1993a, 1993b; Fulton & Trow, 1974; Tuckman, Gapinski, & Hagemann, 1977; Tuckman & Hagemann, 1976), tenure (Boyes, Happel, & Hogan, 1984; Fulton & Trow, 1974; Goodlad, 1990a; Soder, 1989a), and promotion (Allen, 1990; Boyes, Happel, & Hogan, 1984; Fulton & Trow, 1974; Goodlad, 1990a; Moses,

1986; Soder, 1989a). Geographic mobility—the opportunity to move from one university to the other—is discussed as an aspect of the reward structure (Soder, 1989a), but there seems to be no systematic empirical study with a specific focus on geographic mobility. Since the following discussion is to sort out the factors associated with the reward structure in general, the review will cover salary, promotion, and tenure under the rubric of reward structure.

Institutional Variables and the Reward Structure

Institutional type, whether it is distinguished along the public or private dimension, or a scheme similar to Carnegie's classification of higher education institutions (Carnegie Foundation for the Advancement of Teaching, 1987), is usually a variable incorporated into the study design and data analysis, and there is some variance in the reward structure associated with institutional type. For example, Fairweather's study suggests that faculty members' salary increases along the continuum from liberal arts colleges to research universities (1993b); Soder's (1989a) and RATE (AACTE, 1987, 1988, 1990, 1992) studies reveal both similarities and differences in the reward structure across research universities, doctorate granting universities, comprehensive universities, and liberal arts colleges. The general pattern is that research is the most rewarded among all missions, and faculty members want to devote more time to research, but the intensity of the pattern decreases from research universities to liberal arts colleges. Studies with subjects from only one type of institution usually acknowledge the scope of the research. For instance, Long, Allison, and McGinnis (1993), in their inquiry into the role of gender and productivity in rank advancement, state clearly that the data for their study come only from research universities, a statement that implies that the relationship in question might be different across institutional types.

Studies of department leadership within different types of institutions also indicate the association between institutional variables and the reward structure. In Fairweather's (1993a) study, department chairs were asked to rate the relative importance of thirteen factors in granting promotion and tenure. The six top-ranked factors in doctorate granting institutions, which include the Carnegie classifications of research and doctorate granting institutions, are research quality, quality of publications, teaching quality, highest degree, professional reputation, and number of publications. The six top-ranked factors for other four-year institutions include teaching quality, highest degree, fit with department, institutional service, fit with students, and research quality. The rank-order correlation between these two types of institutions is only .38, a coefficient which suggests that according to department chairs' perceptions, the relative importance of various items in the faculty reward structure is different, and there appears to be different patterns of the reward structure in doctorate granting universities and other four-year institutions.

Department size and level of program also affect the reward structure. Boyes, Happel, and Hogan's study of 402 departments of economics (1984) suggests that research is stressed heavily at Ph.D. granting schools and in larger departments, but departments offering only undergraduate degrees and smaller departments emphasize teaching. As a matter of fact, there is some association between institutional type on one hand and department size and level of program on the other—doctorate granting universities usually have larger departments and, by definition, offer higher degrees compared to comprehensive universities and liberal arts colleges. Therefore, it is not surprising to find that studies conducted from the perspectives of institutional type and department characteristics come to the same conclusion, i.e., large departments in doctorate granting institutions put more emphasis on research but less on teaching compared with those relatively small departments in institutions that do not offer doctorates.

Individual Variables and the Reward Structure

According to the literature, individual variables associated with the reward structure include gender, rank, and seniority. Tuckman, Gapinski, and Hagemann (1977) find that the structure of faculty salary differs by gender. Female faculty members earn less than male counterparts with similar characteristics, and the disparity supports the "dual labor market" hypothesis. Long, Allison, and McGinnis (1993) demonstrate that female scientists advance more slowly than male scientists, and few reach full professorship. Allen's (1990) study of senior faculty members in an Australian university suggests that female faculty members are concentrated in the lower rank although they have the same academic qualifications and the same number of publications as their male counterparts. Allen concludes that there appears to be no association between objective measures of academic merit and the speed of promotion or academic rank at a given time and that the general model of success by merit is not supported by the data and analysis. Fairweather's (1993a, 1993b) studies also suggest that the male factor is significantly and positively related to salary. He comments that pay based on gender reflects an irrational and indefensible basis for salary. In short, the studies on association between gender and the reward structure indicate that there are different reward structures for male and female faculty members.

Fairweather's (1993a, pp. 64–65) analysis of compensation by academic rank within types of institutions shows a varied picture of the reward structure:

> Full professors in each type of institution, including comprehensive colleges and liberal arts colleges, are rewarded for publishing and for spending more time on research (and less on teaching). In research universities, doctoral-granting institutions, and comprehensive colleges and universities, associate professors are rewarded for research, administration, teaching, and in one case, service. The earliest point of socialization in the academic career—the assistant professor rank—shows the extent of the research model orientation in American postsecondary education. Producing a substantial publication record and spending more time on research and less on teaching are the dominant factors in compensation for assistant professors.

Moses (1986) inquires into promotion criteria as perceived by professor, reader, senior lecturer, lecturer tenured, lecturer on probation, lecturer on contract, and senior tutor. She concludes that faculty members in lower ranks such as lecturers on probation, lecturers on contract, and senior tutors perceive that involvement in teaching is less rewarded, and they have a strong desire to increase the weight of teaching in promotion criteria.

Disciplines and the Reward Structure

Tuckman and Hagemann's study (1976) suggests that publication is highly rewarded in both education and economics. Economists, however, receive slightly greater remuneration for publication than do those in education. In studying social sciences, liberal arts, math, engineering, biological sciences, and physical sciences, Tuckman, Gapinski, and Hagemann (1977) find that the structure of faculty salary schedules differs by discipline.

Smart and McLaughlin (1978) inquire into the specific differences in the salary structure of the eight clusters of academic disciplines defined by Biglan's three-dimensional (i.e., pure/applied, life/non-life, hard/soft) model of the academic profession. The regression analysis that uses involvement in 11 activities as predictors and salary as the criterion measure, and the rank-order analysis based on the standardized regression coefficients, demonstrate wide variation in the salary structure of the eight discipline clusters.

As the foregoing review suggests, the reward structure differs along some institutional, individual, and disciplinary variables. The literature reviewed so far centers on the determinants of faculty mission involvement and the reward structure, i.e., along which factors faculty members' mission involvement and reward structure differ. The next section of literature review focuses on the relationship between mission involvement and the reward structure.

Evolution of the Institutional Context, Mission, and Faculty of the School of Education

The institutional context has changed for the school of education. The evolution process from normal schools to regional state universities is the very evidence of the changing institutional context for many schools of education. The preparation of teachers used to be the sole or major mission of many higher education institutions, but it now is only one of the missions in the ever growing universities. Particularly during the last quarter-century, there has been a profound shift in the balance of various missions of the school of education. Research has risen to pre-eminence at the expense of teaching and service, including the preparation of teachers.

With the evolution of the institutional context, the school of education has more and more missions. In the United States, the mission of the emergent education professoriate was almost exclusively the preparation of school teachers, a mission which was followed by that of the preparation of school administrators in the beginning of the twentieth century. The education of school teachers and administrators has been further supplemented by the preparation of other educators, such as special educators, school counselors, and school psychologists. Following the development of counselor education after the National Defense Act, the preparation of special educators has gained momentum since 1975, the year of the enactment of the Education for All Handicapped Children Act (PL 94-142).

In addition to educating many kinds of educators, the education professoriate is also expected to provide service to the professional community and the general public, and nowadays are also expected to conduct research (Boyer, 1987; Wisniewski, 1989; Wisniewski & Ducharme, 1989a, 1989b).

Accompanying the expanding mission of the school of education, the education faculty of the school of education became heterogeneous, consisting of several distinguishable groups. James Earl Russell (Hazlett, 1989) and Powell and Sizer (1969) discussed the difference between field- and discipline-oriented professors. Jackson (1975) distinguished disciplinists, generalists, and pedagogists. Still other scholars characterized the education professoriate in different ways (e.g., Clifford & Guthrie, 1988; Ducharme, 1987; Finkelstein, 1982; Judge, 1982; Lawson, 1990; Roemer & Martinello, 1982; Shen, 1995). No matter how the education faculty are categorized in the literature, it is sufficient to conclude that the education professoriate has become diversified.

The Tension between the Diversity of the Institutional Mission and the Unity of the Reward Structure

The changing institutional environment of the school of education, and the accompanying diversification of its missions and the fragmentation of education faculty, raise issues such as whether there is a diversified reward structure to meet the reality in the school of education, a question that the existing literature does not address directly. The existing scholarship on faculty's work and the reward structure focuses on involvement in which mission is most rewarded. Research is perceived to have a very prominent role in the faculty reward structure (e.g., Bok, 1991; Burch, 1989; Carnegie Foundation for the Advancement of Teaching, 1989; Clark, 1987; Lonsdale,

1993; Soderberg, 1985). Involvement in research is found consistently to be positively correlated with reward, whether reward is in the form of pay, promotion, or tenure; involvement in other missions of the school of education is generally not rewarded (Fairweather, 1993a, 1993b).

The basic theme in the literature is that research is heavily rewarded while many other missions are neglected to a certain extent, an observation that raises the issue of how to equitably reward faculty members when the mission is diversified. However, the literature is limited because, in most studies, the reward structure is operationalized as salary, and the studies fail to reveal the dynamic relationship between faculty's work and the reward structure, both of which are multidimensional concepts. For instance, given the importance of research in the reward structure, we still do not know whether the reward structure gives some leeway to faculty members who are heavily involved in missions other than research. This study intends to overcome the foregoing shortcoming in the literature and further our knowledge by studying education faculty members' work and promotion criteria, both of which are operationalized as multidimensional concepts.

Given the paramount importance of research in the reward structure as illustrated in past studies, is there a set of Procrustean, unified, and homogeneous promotion criteria for every faculty member? Or a common core of promotion criteria with some leeway depending on an individual faculty member's work? We do not know much about whether there is a common core in the promotion criteria, i.e., some important criteria along which every member should be judged. Fulton and Trow (1974, p. 67) made the following comment on the basis of their study of faculty research productivity in different types of institutions:

> We are suggesting that in the leading (and doubtless some medium-quality) universities, the academic role includes the expectation of continuing research activity; in weaker universities and strong colleges there is the expectation (and acceptance) that the role may or may not include active research work; while in the middle-level and other colleges, research is not a normal expectation of the academic role.

It would be interesting to inquire into Fulton and Trow's comment on whether research constitutes a core for different types of institutions, and to inquire further into whether other missions comprise the common core. Questions of this nature can be studied only by inquiring into various aspects of mission involvement and promotion criteria.

Although it is important to inquire into mission involvement and promotion criteria along the line of the existing literature, it is also crucial to probe into whether there is a set of diversified promotion criteria in the school of education. This chapter intends to inquire into whether the promotion criteria take into account levels and patterns of faculty members' involvement in the nine missions of the school of education that have been defined in the previous chapters, and to explore whether the relationship between mission involvement and promotion criteria varies for faculty members in research universities, doctorate granting universities, and comprehensive universities as defined by the Carnegie Foundation (1987).

The inquiry in this chapter has two research questions. First, do faculty members with *different levels of involvement* in a certain mission of the school of education perceive differently the weight of this mission in current and desired promotion criteria? If so, how do they differ? Second, do faculty members with *different patterns of involvement* in missions of the school of education perceive current and desired promotion criteria differently? If so, how do they differ? In other words, what is the canonical correlation between faculty members' current mission involvement and current promotion criteria, and between current mission involvement and desired promotion criteria? As will be discussed in detail later, the question on the level of mission involvement inquires into how faculty members perceive their levels of involvement in a certain mission and *this* mission's weight in promotion criteria. Therefore, the first question is a bivariate inquiry into the faculty's mission involvement and promotion criteria. The second question, however, takes into account the relationship among involvement in the nine missions—i.e., patterns of mission involvement such as high involvement in research but low involvement in all the others—and inquires into how faculty members with different patterns of mission involvement perceive the promotion criteria. Therefore, the second question is a multivariate inquiry into mission involvement and promotion criteria.

The analysis in this chapter differs from previous scholarship in that it defines both mission involvement and promotion criteria as multidimensional entities and then explores the relationship between the two multidimensional concepts. Most past studies use salary as the criterion measure, a variable that cannot be articulated in terms of the various possible missions of the school of education. By inquiring into how education faculty members are involved in the nine missions, and how these nine missions are important for promotion purposes, we are able to reveal a dynamic picture regarding the relationship between mission involvement and promotion criteria.

The nature of the promotion criteria in relation to faculty members' levels and patterns of involvement has great implications for the health and well-being of the school of education. Promotion criteria that do not take into consideration faculty members' levels and patterns of mission involvement marginalize some of the missions of the school of education, hurt faculty members' morale, and ultimately hinder institutional health. An inquiry into the nature of the promotion criteria in relation to faculty members' levels and patterns of mission involvement will further our understanding of the complexity of the issue and provide a knowledge base to consider the policy issues involved.

As described in chapter 5, faculty members were asked to rate their *current involvement* in the nine missions of the school of education on a Likert scale, ranging from 1 (not at all involved), to 2 (marginally involved), 3 (moderately involved), and 4 (heavily involved). Second, respondents were asked to rate the *current* weight placed by their institution on each of the missions of the school of education for promotion on a Likert scale, ranging from 1 (not considered), to 2 (marginally helpful), 3 (moderately helpful), and 4 (essential). Finally, respondents were asked to indicate, by using the same scale as their responses to the current promotion criteria, the *desired* weight for promotion that should be placed on each of the missions.

Consistent with the two research questions, there are two approaches to data analysis. The first approach is to inquire into how the high- and low-involvement groups in a certain mission perceive the corresponding mission's weight in promotion criteria. Whether the weights are unified or diversified could be discerned by studying means of the high- and low-involvement groups and the difference between the two groups. Respondents were asked to rate their current involvement in each of the nine missions of the school of education on a Likert scale, ranging from 1 (not at all involved) to 4 (heavily involved). Respondents who rated their involvement as 1 or 2 are coded into the low-involvement group, while those who reported 3 and 4 are coded into the high-involvement group. Therefore, there are high- and low-involvement groups for each of the nine missions, and an individual faculty member might belong to the high-involvement group in teaching but to the low-involvement group in research.

The second approach is to inquire into whether faculty members with different patterns of mission involvement perceive the promotion criteria differently. The result of the canonical analysis will not only suggest the nature of the canonical correlation but also the diversity or unity of current and desired promotion criteria.

Unity of Promotion Criteria
as Reflected in the Quantitative Survey Data

Current and Desired Promotion Criteria

Table 6.1 reports mission items' weights in current and desired promotion criteria as perceived by the high- and low-involvement groups of faculty members in research, doctorate granting, and comprehensive universities. The statistics included are the means of the low- and high-involvement groups, and the mean difference between the two groups. A note is needed here regarding statistical significance versus practical significance (Stevens, 1992, pp. 9–12). Because power is heavily dependent on sample size and the samples in this study are fairly large, in most cases null hypotheses are easily rejected at the .05 level. Therefore, the focus is on the absolute value of the mean difference between the high- and low-involvement groups.

The analyses of the high- and low-involvement groups' perceptions of current and desired promotion criteria, as illustrated in Table 6.1, reveal some strong patterns and interesting findings. First, there is a difference between the high-involvement groups' perception of current and desired promotion criteria. The high-involvement groups perceive that only research and, in some cases, teaching, have average weights greater than 3.0 in current promotion criteria, and

Table 6.1

Mission Items' Weights in Current and Desired Promotion Criteria as Perceived by the High- and Low-Involvement Groups
of Faculty Members in Research, Doctorate Granting, and Comprehensive Universities

	Research university			Doctorate granting university			Comprehensive university		
	Mlow	Mhigh	Mh-Ml	Mlow	Mhigh	Mh-Ml	Mlow	Mhigh	Mh-Ml
Items in current promotion criteria									
Teaching	2.76 *	2.82 **	0.06 ***	3.35	3.26	-0.09	3.53	3.43	-0.10
Research and scholarly activity	3.72	3.93	0.21	3.65	3.62	-0.03	3.53	3.46	-0.07
Development, dissemination, and demonstration	2.12	2.47	0.35	2.29	2.66	0.37	2.48	2.81	0.33
Ad hoc services to schools	1.90	1.98	0.08	2.30	2.42	0.12	2.50	2.56	0.06
Effecting change in public schools	1.65	1.88	0.23	1.73	2.00	0.27	1.83	2.26	0.43
Preparation of school teachers	2.03	2.37	0.34	2.45	2.68	0.23	2.47	2.93	0.46
Preparation of special educators	1.98	2.39	0.41	2.35	2.73	0.38	2.42	2.87	0.45
Preparation of school administrators	2.02	2.37	0.35	2.45	2.64	0.19	2.21	2.91	0.07
Preparation of researchers and/or university faculty	2.71	2.84	0.13	2.20	2.50	0.30	1.83	2.23	0.04
Items in desired promotion criteria									
Teaching	3.54	3.77	0.23	3.89	3.79	0.10	3.67	3.87	0.20
Research and scholarly activity	3.38	3.65	0.27	2.98	3.49	0.51	2.84	3.42	0.58
Development, dissemination, and demonstration	2.64	3.08	0.44	2.51	3.07	0.56	2.64	3.19	0.55
Ad hoc services to schools	2.38	2.91	0.53	2.42	3.14	0.72	2.54	3.11	0.57
Effecting change in public schools	2.62	3.17	0.55	2.46	3.08	0.62	2.50	3.24	0.74
Preparation of school teachers	2.98	3.42	0.44	2.83	3.42	0.59	2.88	3.57	0.69
Preparation of special educators	2.49	3.09	0.60	2.49	3.40	0.91	2.53	3.53	1.00
Preparation of school administrators	2.53	3.11	0.58	2.53	3.27	0.74	2.34	3.22	0.88
Preparation of researchers and/or university faculty	2.86	3.41	0.55	2.36	3.08	0.72	2.12	2.76	0.64

*read as in research universities, the low-involvement group in teaching perceives teaching has an average weight of 2.76 in current promotion criteria.

**read as in research universities, the high-involvement group in teaching perceives teaching has an average weight of 2.82 in current promotion criteria.

***read as the mean difference of teaching's weight in current promotion criteria as perceived by the high- and low-involvement groups in teaching is 0.06.

that the rest of the missions all have weights less than 3.0. This indicates that according to the respondents' perceptions, involvement in missions other than teaching and research is not rewarded in accordance with the level of involvement. The high-involvement groups' perception of desired promotion criteria reveals a different picture. With only two exceptions, the high-involvement groups indicate that each of the missions that they are involved in should have a weight greater than 3.0, revealing a desire that heavy involvement in any mission of the school of education should be highly rewarded. According to the high-involvement groups' perception, in current promotion criteria there seems to be a cap on the weight of missions other than research and teaching; and they want to remove the cap. For the missions other than teaching and research, both high- and low-involvement groups perceive that these missions have average weights less than 3.0 in current promotion criteria, which implies that these missions are, to a certain extent, marginalized.

Second, for missions other than teaching, the differences between the perceptions of the high- and low-involvement groups are twice as large for desired promotion criteria as for current promotion criteria. In other words, the mean differences between the high- and low-involvement groups are greater for desired promotion criteria than for current promotion criteria. This phenomenon indicates faculty members' desire to have more diversified weights in association with their levels of involvement, with high-involvement groups desiring to have higher weights. Furthermore, this phenomenon also confirms the pattern discussed in the previous paragraph—the high-involvement groups desire that involvement in any mission of the school of education should be rewarded to the level of involvement, while the low-involvement groups do not desire this. Teaching is the only exception to the foregoing generalization. As will be discussed in the next paragraph, this is because teaching constitutes the common core in desired promotion criteria and, therefore, there is little difference between the perceptions of high- and low-involvement groups.

Third, there is a desire on the part of faculty members in all three types of institutions to have a shift from the current more research-oriented promotion criteria to the desired more teaching-oriented ones. If we define the common core of the promotion criteria as those missions that both the high- and low-involvement groups involved in such missions perceive as having average weights greater than 3.0, the common core of promotion criteria as perceived by faculty members in research, doctorate granting, and comprehensive universities can be summarized in Table 6.2. On one hand, research appears to be the common core of *current* promotion criteria for all groups of faculty members. On the other hand, teaching is the common core of *desired* promotion criteria for all groups of faculty members. The general trend here is that there seems to be a desire for a shift of emphasis from research to teaching for promotion purposes.

Table 6.2

A Summary of the Common Core in Current and Desired Promotion Criteria as Perceived by Faculty Members in Research, Doctorate Granting, and Comprehensive Universities

Faculty group	Current Promotion Criteria		Desired Promotion Criteria	
	Teaching	Research	Teaching	Research
RU		common core	common core	common core
DGU	common core	common core	common core	
CU	common core	common core	common core	

The foregoing discussion on the common core uses 3.0 as the cut-off point for defining common core. Although 3.0 has its meaning based on the 4-point scale, it is, to a certain degree, arbitrary. However, the observation arising from comparing the common core— a desire for a shift of emphasis from research to teaching for promotion purposes—is supported by the average weights of teaching and research perceived by the high- and low-involvement groups (Table 6.1). Except for faculty members in comprehensive universities for whom the weights of teaching and research are more balanced, for all other groups of faculty members research has much higher weights than teaching in current promotion criteria. The gap between teaching and research is particularly conspicuous for faculty members in research universities. However, where desired promotion criteria are concerned, the focus that research receives in current promotion criteria shifts to teaching. All groups of faculty members, regardless of their levels of involvement in teaching, perceive that teaching should have average weights greater than or equal to 3.5. Furthermore, for all groups of faculty members, the desired weights for teaching are greater than those for research. All these indicate that education faculty members want to change the current research-oriented promotion criteria to the desired teaching-oriented promotion criteria.

In short, the analyses presented in the foregoing suggest that there is a unity in current promotion criteria that gives rise to the discrepancy between education faculty members' mission involvement and promotion criteria. The unity and discrepancy are reflected in the following. First, except for the common-core missions, the mean differences between the high- and low-involvement groups are greater for desired promotion criteria than for current promotion criteria. Education faculty members desire to have a set of more diversified weights consistent with their levels of involvement in the missions of the school of education. Second, in current promotion criteria, there seems to be a ceiling on the weights of missions other than teaching and research, and the high-involvement groups want to have the ceiling removed. In other words, high-involvement in any mission of the school of education should deserve high reward. Finally, there is a discrepancy between the faculty's teaching-oriented mission involvement and the current research-dominated promotion criteria, and their desire to have a set of more teaching-oriented promotion criteria to be consistent with their priority of current mission involvement.

Canonical Correlation between Current Mission Involvement and Current Promotion Criteria, and between Current Mission Involvement and Desired Promotion Criteria

Tables 6.3 to 6.5 summarize the canonical correlation analyses. Only canonical variates with canonical correlation coefficients greater than or equal to .3 are displayed. So are the item loadings of the canonical variate. The following patterns reveal a strong desire on the part of all three faculty groups to align promotion criteria with their patterns of mission involvement. First, the number of pairs of canonical variates is greater for the canonical correlation between current mission involvement and desired promotion criteria than for the canonical correlation between current mission involvement and current promotion criteria. The number of canonical variates ranges from three to four pairs for the canonical correlation between current mission involvement and current promotion criteria, while the number

Table 6.3

*Canonical Correlation between Current Mission Involvement
and Current and Desired Promotion Criteria for Faculty Members in Research Universities*

Items	Canonical Variates and Loadings							
	Current Involvement			Current Involvement				
	1	2	3	1	2	3	4	5
Teaching	0.39			-0.31		-0.32		
Research and scholarly activity		0.40			0.38			
Development, dissemination, and demonstration	0.35		-0.45				0.81	-0.43
Ad hoc services to schools and other agencies		0.32	-0.35	-0.42			0.77	0.52
Effecting changes in public schools		0.53					0.61	
Preparation of school teachers	0.65	0.50	0.56	-0.70		-0.49		
Preparation of special educators	0.34		0.33		-0.39	0.52		
Preparation of school administrators	-0.42		0.44	0.63			0.40	
Preparation of researchers and/or college faculty		0.54			0.75			
Proportion of raw variance explained	*0.14*	*0.14*	*0.13*	*0.17*	*0.11*	*0.11*	*0.19*	*0.06*
Redundancy	*0.04*	*0.03*	*0.02*	*0.05*	*0.03*	*0.02*	*0.03*	*0.01*
Items	Current Promotion Criteria			Desired Promotion Criteria				
Teaching		0.60				-0.52		
Research and scholarly activity					0.67			
Development, dissemination, and demonstration	0.50			-0.41			0.82	
Ad hoc services to schools and other agencies	0.33			0.34			0.81	
Effecting changes in public schools			0.54				0.52	
Preparation of school teachers	0.30		0.60	-0.30		-0.38		
Preparation of special educators	0.42		0.36			0.43		0.56
Preparation of school administrators				0.37				0.42
Preparation of researchers and/or college faculty				0.69				
Proportion of raw variance explained	*0.09*	*0.04*	*0.11*	*0.06*	*0.10*	*0.07*	*0.19*	*0.10*
Redundancy	*0.03*	*0.01*	*0.02*	*0.02*	*0.03*	*0.02*	*0.03*	*0.01*
Canonical correlation	*0.56*	*0.46*	*0.38*	*0.55*	*0.52*	*0.49*	*0.39*	*0.32*

Table 6.4

Canonical Correlation between Current Mission Involvement and Current and Desired Promotion Criteria for Faculty Members in Doctorate Granting Universities

Current Involvement

Items	Canonical Variates and Loadings					
	Current Involvement			Current Involvement		
	1	2	3	4	5	6
Teaching	0.74			−0.38		
Research and scholarly activity		−0.36				
Development, dissemination, and demonstration	−0.42	0.46	0.60	0.61	0.35	0.55
Ad hoc services to schools and other agencies	−0.30	0.42	0.31	0.44	0.40	0.37
Effecting changes in public schools	−0.42	0.54	0.47	0.47	−0.40	0.41
Preparation of school teachers		−0.49	−0.47		0.32	0.35
Preparation of special educators		0.53			0.66	
Preparation of school administrators						
Preparation of researchers and/or college faculty	0.61					
Proportion of raw variance explained	*0.16*	*0.16*	*0.11*	*0.13*	*0.13*	*0.11*
Redundancy	*0.07*	*0.05*	*0.03*	*0.03*	*0.02*	*0.01*

Current Promotion Criteria / Desired Promotion Criteria

Items	Current Promotion Criteria			Desired Promotion Criteria		
	1	2	3	4	5	6
Teaching	−0.38		0.80	0.69	0.57	0.50
Research and scholarly activity	0.63		0.43			0.63
Development, dissemination, and demonstration	−0.53	0.36	0.44	0.37		0.56
Ad hoc services to schools and other agencies		0.42	0.32	0.31		
Effecting changes in public schools	−0.46		0.40	0.43	0.39	0.61
Preparation of school teachers	−0.30	−0.43	0.64	0.31	0.63	0.51
Preparation of special educators		0.33	0.49	0.47		
Preparation of school administrators	0.48	0.09				
Preparation of researchers and/or college faculty						
Proportion of raw variance explained	*0.16*	*0.03*	*0.24*	*0.16*	*0.13*	*0.21*
Redundancy	*0.07*	*0.03*	*0.03*	*0.03*	*0.02*	*0.02*
Canonical correlation	*0.58*	*0.45*	*0.33*	*0.45*	*0.37*	*0.30*

Table 6.5

Canonical Correlation between Current Mission Involvement and Current and Desired Promotion Criteria for Faculty Members in Comprehensive Universities

Canonical Variates and Loadings

Items	Current Involvement				Current Involvement					
	1	2	3	4	1	2	3	4	5	6
Teaching										
Research and scholarly activity		0.45	0.30	-0.44	-0.36		0.66			-0.31
Development, dissemination, and demonstration		0.61			0.31		0.60	0.44	0.42	
Ad hoc services to schools and other agencies		0.61			0.48		0.53	-0.33		
Effecting changes in public schools		0.65	0.40	0.64	0.50		0.55	-0.32	0.42	
Preparation of school teachers	-0.43	0.34			0.42	0.33				
Preparation of special educators	-0.48		0.57		0.41	0.70			-0.48	
Preparation of school administrators	0.52		0.66	0.36			0.58			0.40
Preparation of researchers and/or college faculty	0.30	0.73			-0.37	0.44	0.51			0.47
Proportion of raw variance explained	*0.11*	*0.24*	*0.15*	*0.09*	*0.15*	*0.14*	*0.23*	*0.07*	*0.12*	*0.07*
Redundancy	*0.04*	*0.05*	*0.02*	*0.01*	*0.06*	*0.05*	*0.04*	*0.01*	*0.02*	*0.01*

Items	Current Promotion Criteria				Desired Promotion Criteria					
	1	2	3	4	1	2	3	4	5	6
Teaching			0.44	-0.38	-0.47				0.39	-0.36
Research and scholarly activity		0.51		0.47	0.43		0.38	0.44	0.33	
Development, dissemination, and demonstration					0.55		0.50		0.38	
Ad hoc services to schools and other agencies		0.55	0.49		0.46		0.36		0.48	
Effecting changes in public schools			0.48	0.49	0.72		0.58			
Preparation of school teachers				0.33	0.61	0.46			-0.37	
Preparation of special educators			0.77	0.61	0.31					
Preparation of school administrators	0.51	0.77	0.49				0.54	0.49		0.45
Preparation of researchers and/or college faculty						0.51	0.39			0.49
Proportion of raw variance explained	*0.06*	*0.16*	*0.22*	*0.15*	*0.22*	*0.09*	*0.18*	*0.09*	*0.11*	*0.09*
Redundancy	*0.02*	*0.03*	*0.03*	*0.02*	*0.08*	*0.03*	*0.03*	*0.01*	*0.01*	*0.01*
Canonical correlation	*0.56*	*0.44*	*0.38*	*0.32*	*0.61*	*0.59*	*0.43*	*0.40*	*0.37*	*0.33*

of canonical variates varies from five to six pairs for the canonical correlation between current mission involvement and desired promotion criteria. On average, the number of pairs of variates for canonical correlation between current mission involvement and current promotion criteria is 3.3 pairs, in contrast to 5.7 pairs for the canonical correlation between current mission involvement and desired promotion criteria. Second, as the other side of the same picture revealed in the number of pairs of canonical variates, the canonical correlation coefficients for current mission involvement and desired promotion criteria are greater than those for current mission involvement and current promotion criteria. Finally, the canonical correlation variates between current mission involvement and desired promotion criteria are more interpretable than those between current mission involvement and current promotion criteria.

The canonical analyses reveal faculty members' desire to diversify promotion criteria and to align promotion criteria with their patterns of involvement in the missions of the school of education. Because of the diversification of missions of the school of education, the issue of diversification of promotion criteria is more urgent than ever. Suppose there are two faculty members in a research university: one is heavily involved in teaching, research, and the preparation of teachers, and the other is heavily involved in teaching, research, and the preparation of school administrators. The difference in mission involvement between these two faculty members is that one is involved in the preparation of school teachers, the other in the preparation of school administrators. The analysis in this section reveals that in addition to being rewarded for involvement in teaching and research, the first faculty member also wishes to be rewarded for involvement in the preparation of school teachers, while the second desires to be rewarded for involvement in the preparation of school administrators. There is a need and a desire for a set of diversified promotion criteria to suit faculty members' patterns of involvement in missions of the school of education.

In contrast to canonical correlation analyses on current mission involvement and desired promotion criteria, analyses on current mission involvement and current promotion criteria suggest that there is currently a set of more unified, homogeneous, and Procrustean promotion criteria. Therefore, tension exists between the current Procrustean promotion criteria and the desired diversified ones. This tension will become more critical as the missions of the school of education continue to diversify.

The canonical analyses confirm some of the previous findings from the analyses of high- and low-involvement groups, in which the high-involvement groups desire that the corresponding missions should have higher weights in desired promotion criteria. The analysis of the high- and low-involvement groups is bivariate. The canonical correlation analysis, by showing that there is more association between current mission involvement and desired promotion criteria than between current mission involvement and current promotion criteria, supports the results of bivariate analysis from a multivariate perspective.

Unity of Promotion Criteria
as Reflected in Qualitative Interview Data

The interview data regarding faculty members in the school of education also reveal that there is a unity in the promotion criteria. The emphasis is on research and many other aspects of the education faculty's work are neglected to a great extent:

> The reward structure is more rigid. There's more emphasis on research and publications. Our dean favors those who do research and get grants. There's a tendency to look for new people with long publication lists. Depends on who is on the selection committee. The younger faculty are really torn apart—role demands from above versus doing a good job with preservice. The Stanford or Berkeley people who come here are much more oriented toward research. (Male, Professor of Science Education, 28 years)

> Now, it's generate dollars, which will translate into research where publications will accrue. Fifteen years ago, getting tenure and promotion was like high schools—letter in the mail, congratulations. Last dozen years is when the publishing and research emphasis changed. (Male, Associate Professor of Agriculture, 6 years)

> Absolutely publish. I don't think it's changed. Other people will say that it has. They were told, they say, that teaching and service were equally important, but I don't think so. Teaching is not even an evaluation category. (Female, Associate Professor of Curriculum and Instruction, 18 years)

I know how to do research, mind you, got my doctorate in research and statistics, and I've a pretty fair reputation as a researcher, but now what we're doing is considered lesser quality, you know, like the only people who can do research are the people in the ed psych area and what we do is second-rate somehow. They don't tell you that directly, but that's the implication. We have unheard-of loads here. It's almost as if they are planning to get rid of us, because we have so much to do that we can't possibly do it all well, and then they'll have their justification to eliminate us. The pupil teacher ratio in two of the areas is 40–1, but in ed psych, it's 15–1. (Male, Professor of Science Education, 20 years)

Research is valued very highly, of course, but some of us have an easier time of it than others. The foundations people aren't struggling with the problems we have, so they have much more time. The ed psych people have a service course or two, but that's all. We have to go after our own money, and we are doing it, we are getting the money. (Female, Professor of Special Education, 16 years)

The combination of the emphasis on research and the unity of the promotion criteria has serious impacts on the school of education and its faculty. Some faculty members discussed the resultant low morale:

It sure helps to get money around here, let me tell you. The dean likes NSF grants, that's the real reward structure. You gotta publish if you want to make it, but it's a whole lot better if you can snare some NSF money. Didn't used to be that way. There was a time when they hired all sorts of people. Research was okay, but not so damned big like it is now, and there are lots of young faculty who are worried—morale is piss poor because they are worried and at the same time there's a lot of senior faculty—not me, mind you—but a lot of senior faculty who are sitting around on their cans and you know they wouldn't make it today, but there they are. (Male, Associate Professor of Educational Psychology, 21 years)

When I came here, it was a totally teaching institution, when I came here in 1968, and that's *why* I came here, because I wanted to teach. There was a shift to research and publishing, which was tied to notions of merit pay. After all, teaching is hard to judge, all they had were student ratings, which you don't want to rely on anyway. So I think the two are connected, merit pay and the push for research. As a result of the change, we have had very poor morale, especially among the older faculty. There was a time when you got riffed if you hadn't published an article in the past 3 years. It was a stinking situation, everybody distrustful, people all of a sudden feeling they were in competition with colleagues, really a stinky scene. (Male, Professor of Educational Foundations, 20 years)

Some faculty members resent the fact that when research becomes more and more important in promotion criteria, teacher education has been neglected:

The President doesn't give a shit about the teacher education program here. He doesn't give a shit about it. He wants the glamour of research and research money. (Male, Professor of History, 20 years)

The sole emphasis on research, which is perceived as individual work by many faculty members, takes a toll on collective work, such as developing and strengthening programs:

We don't look at the nature of schooling, the nature of people, as we should. There's no sense of purpose. Courses are just a hodgepodge that grew like Topsy. We're plugging holes in dams. Individual professors will deal with effective schools or moral imperatives of teaching. But there's no framework. Each course is its own main program. The reason for this lack of framework is clear—there's no reward for working on an overall program. (Female, Associate Professor of Curriculum and Instruction, 18 years)

The promotion criteria, with sole emphasis on research, also create tension between the junior and senior faculty members. Senior faculty members are angry with the changed promotion criteria because the work they used to do is not valued as much any more. Junior faculty members take a different approach to their professional work because of the "publish or perish" pressure, and they resent the fact that they are now judged by those senior faculty members who probably would not have made it under the current criteria. The following are excerpts from the interviews with faculty members:

The reward structure is as elsewhere. It changed, just about the time I got here, to (a) publish or perish, (b) politics and the old boy network and how well you get along with certain people, and (c) teaching, sort of. That is to say, you'd best not be a really lousy teacher. But it's publishing first and foremost. There are serious clashes as a result of this shift from the old reward structure (which was teacher plus service) and it's been tough for some of the older folks. They feel threatened by those of us who do scholarly work. There are clashes on search committees between those who are looking for researchers and scholars and those who just want to hire some good little teachers. (Male, Associate Professor of Elementary Education, 6 years)

The new hires, here and in arts and sciences, are hired on the basis of ability to do research. I was one of the first people brought in with some sort of research background in mind. There's a lot of tension between the old timers and the more recent hires. (Male, Professor of Educational Psychology, 12 years)

There were a lot of high powered research oriented new faculty here, at a time when there was overproduction of Ph.D.'s. [The dean] allied himself with the Stanford and Berkeley crowd—the people who thought they were just going to be here for a few years anyway, they were using this place as a stepping stone to better research universities. (Male, Professor of Educational Foundations, 20 years)

Once you are over the bar, you can crash. No more rewards. But once *they've* cleared the bar, their memories have fogged. They think the bar is at 17 feet or whatever when it wasn't anywhere near that high. (Male, Associate Professor of Educational Psychology, 12 years)

Right now, we don't know what our mission is. There are lots of people who have been here 20–25 years. They were elementary school teachers before that. They haven't grown. They still think they are in public school. (Male, Professor of Secondary Education, 14 years)

Some of the junior faculty members feel that the change of the reward structure does not come in tandem with the support system. The requirement for research has been increased, but other kinds of responsibilities are not reduced:

Publishing and grants are much more important. This definitely has been a change in the last 10 years. It used to be quality teaching as the norm. Now it is research, still some teaching. The teaching load is 4 courses a semester. No reductions. Lots of pressure. There's no support, no time to do a good job. It used to be teaching only, publications and grants were feathers in the cap. Now it's shifting and people are pissed, no help, no travel. (Male, Associate Professor of Math Education, 8 years)

Some senior members are resentful of the changed promotion criteria, but they are not willing to budge:

When I came here, it was teaching and community involvement. I got promoted that way. Now they want to make [research] an important item. Every time we get a new dean or vice president for academic affairs they make a big deal about research. Sometimes it seems they would like to have everything. I'll retire as an associate professor because I won't sacrifice my teaching for research. (Female, Associate Professor of Psychology, 16 years)

[In speaking of a favorite project, one involving numerous professors over the years:] With the president's emphasis on research, a lot of faculty who had been glad to pitch in on [the project] all of a sudden found they didn't have the time, where's the payoff? they said. I guess I can't blame them. I'm a full professor. You can't teach an old dog new tricks, and like I said, I came here because I wanted to teach, and I was hired to teach and that's what I'm going to continue to do. (Male, Professor of Educational Foundations, 20 years)

Summary

Both the quantitative survey data and the qualitative interview data indicate that the common core of current promotion criteria is more research-oriented, and faculty members desire that the common core be teaching-focused. The common core essentially reflects the identity and future of the school of education. Therefore, the faculty members in schools of education have shown their dissatisfaction with the current predominance of research in current promotion criteria and with the projected future of the school of education.

Both quantitative and qualitative data also suggest that there is a set of unified and Procrustean promotion criteria in the school of education. No matter how education faculty members are involved in the missions, they are basically judged by the same set of promotion criteria, which are heavily weighted toward research. Therefore, there are two contradictions associated with the Procrustean promotion criteria. First, given the fact that today faculty members have multi-dimensional missions, the Procrustean promotion criteria will ultimately emphasize some missions while neglecting others. Second, the Procrustean promotion criteria are also unfair to those faculty members whose mission involvement is not consistent with that of the current promotion criteria. As illustrated in the interview data, there is a strong resentment among some faculty members.

The analysis and discussion in this chapter raise an important question as to how to equitably reward education faculty members. The current Procrustean one seems to have gone to an extreme. The crucial point here is how to develop a reward structure in which involvement in any legitimate mission of the school of education is rewarded to the level of involvement, an issue that will be further discussed in the final chapter.

CHAPTER SEVEN

Faculty Fragmentation and Teacher Education

As discussed in chapters one and two, many of the teacher preparation institutions evolved from normal schools to teachers' colleges to state colleges and to regional state universities. This transition, virtually completed by the early 1970s, was accompanied by a severe loss of identity of teacher education (Goodlad, 1990a; Howey & Zimpher, 1990). Teacher education, once the only mission of these institutions, is now just *one* of the many businesses in these multi-purpose institutions (Cohen, Birnbaum, Pfnister, & Geiger, 1985; Kerr, 1994).

Along with the evolution of many teacher education institutions is the increase of the importance of research in the faculty's reward system (e.g., Bok, 1991; Burch, 1989; Carnegie Foundation for the Advancement of Teaching, 1989; Ducharme & Kluender, 1990; Lawson, 1990). From his interviews in 29 colleges and universities, Soder (1989a, 1989b, 1990b) finds that a shift from teaching to research is present in all schools of education, although there is variance among flagship public, major public, regional public, major private, regional private, and liberal arts, with flagship public and major private universities at one end of the continuum and liberal arts colleges at the other.

With the rising importance of research in the reward structure, a two-tier system of researchers and clinicians has been developed in schools of education (Clifford & Guthrie, 1988; Lanier & Little, 1986). The development of the two-tier system is associated with the change of the origin of education faculty from practitioner-turned-professors to practitioner-scholars and to professional education scholars (Lawson, 1990). This two-tier system within schools of education erodes the effectiveness of the preparation of teachers (Clifford & Guthrie, 1988; Darling-Hammond, 1994; Goodlad, 1990a, 1990b).

Although the conceptualization of the two-tier system is perhaps simplistic due to its dichotomous nature, it captures the essence of the "fragmentation" of the education faculty as discussed by Lawson (1990, p. 62) and Wisniewski and Ducharme (1989a, p. 6). The aforementioned studies contribute greatly to the understanding of education faculty, the reward structure, and teacher education. However, we do not know the degree to which faculty fragmentation has developed in schools of education. We know even less about the degree of impact this fragmentation has had, and will have, on teacher education, which used to be the sole mission of the school of education. This chapter addresses these questions by conducting analyses of quantitative survey data and qualitative interview data from the Study of Education of Educators and draws some implications for the school of education and teacher education in the future.

Fragmentation of the Faculty in the School of Education

The survey respondents were asked to rate their current involvement in teaching, research, the preparation of school teachers, and other missions of the school of education (please refer to the appendix for a detailed description of the sample). Of the respondents, 16.1% report that they have no involvement in the preparation of school teachers, 13.6% are marginally involved, 17.0% are moderately involved, and 53.3% are heavily involved. If the percentages of the "not-at-all involved" and "marginally involved" groups are added, nearly 30% of the education faculty has little or no involvement in the preparation of school teachers. Given the fact that the preparation of school teachers used to be the sole mission of the school of education, this percentage suggests that the education faculty has become fragmented in its missions.

Table 7.1

*Correlation between Current Involvement in the Preparation of Teachers
and Other Missions of the School of Education*

Other missions of the school of education	Correlation with preparation of teachers
Teaching	.3250**
Research and scholarly activity	-.0821**
Development, dissemination, and demonstration	.1568**
Ad hoc services to schools and other educational agencies	.1913**
Effecting changes in public schools	.2407**
Professional preparation of special educators	.1879**
Professional preparation of school administrators	-.0965**
Preparation of researchers and/or university/college faculty	-.0543

** $p < .01$ (two-tailed).

For the purpose of testing the hypothesis of fragmentation of the education faculty, the respondents were asked to rate their current involvement in missions of the school of education on a 4-point scale with increasing involvement, and Pearson's correlation coefficients between current involvement in the preparation of school teachers and other missions of the school of education were computed (Table 7.1). Two observations can be made from Table 7.1. First, involvement in preparation of teachers has a negative correlation with research and scholarly activity. Faculty members who are more involved in the preparation of teachers are less likely to engage in research and scholarly productivity. Second, the education faculty's involvement in the preparation of school teachers has positive correlations with teaching, services to schools, and effecting changes in public schools. Faculty members who are more involved in the preparation of teachers participate more in those teaching- and service-related activities. These two observations do not address whether engagement in research enhances or impedes the effectiveness of teaching (Feldman, 1987). Rather, they illustrate the correlations between current involvement in the preparation of school teachers and other missions of the school of education, and they support the hypothesis of fragmentation of the education faculty.

In order to further test the aforementioned observation that the education faculty is fragmented in its missions, three discriminant function analyses were conducted to inquire into whether the four groups ranging from not-at-all involved to heavily involved in the preparation of school teachers could be statistically discriminated against their perceived and desired missions for the school of education.

Discriminant function analysis is developed for two purposes: describing major differences among groups and classifying subjects into groups on the basis of a set of criterion measures. The discriminant function analyses conducted in the following were to describe the major differences among the groups. Discriminant function analysis has a nice feature of "parsimony of description" because, for instance, in comparing 5 groups on 10 variables, we may find that the groups differ primarily on only two major dimensions, i.e., the discriminant functions (Stevens, 1992, pp. 273–274). As will be discussed, the dimension can be properly named by studying the loadings of the criterion measures on the discriminant function.

The discriminant function analyses conducted in this study are direct discriminant function analyses in which, like standard multiple regression, all predictors enter the equations at once and each predictor is assigned only the unique association it has with groups. Variance shared among predictors contributes to the total relationship, but not to any one predictor.

Standard (direct) discriminant function analyses were performed to find the dimension or dimensions along which the four groups differ. In order to find out possible patterns with which the groups differ, standard discriminant function analyses were conducted on faculty's perceived support for the missions of the school of education and their perceived and desirable weights of these missions for tenure consideration. The respondents were asked to rate the aforementioned factors on a 7-point scale with increasing importance. The significant discriminant functions are reported in Table 7.2.

The loading matrix of correlations between predictors and discriminant functions suggests that the discriminant functions in all three analyses are basically a dimension of teaching and the preparation of school educators (including school teachers, special educators, and school administrators). The four groups as a whole differ along this dimension. By looking carefully at group centroids, we may find that the heavily involved group differs from the other three groups. The group centroids further illustrate how the difference

Table 7.2

Results of Discriminant Function Analyses[a]

Predictor variables	Perceived support for the following missions	Correlations of predictors and discriminant functions	
		Perceived weight of the following for tenure	Desirable weight of the following for tenure
Teaching	.83	.39	.50
Research and scholarly activity	.04	-.04	-.26
Development, dissemination, and demonstration	.44	.68	.31
Ad hoc services to schools and other educational agencies	.30	.44	.42
Effecting changes in public schools	.27	.31	.32
Professional preparation of school teachers	.83	.74	.81
Professional preparation of special educators	.59	.45	.22
Professional preparation of school administrators	.40	.20	.04
Preparation of researchers and/or university/college faculty	.05	-.07	-.13
Variability accounted and eigenvalue			
Between-group variability accounted	.68	.84	.84
Within-group variability accounted (canonical R)	.30	.34	.39
Eigenvalue	.08	.14	.18
Group centroids			
Not-at-all involved	-.32	-.52	-.58
Marginally involved	-.41	-.43	-.55
Moderately involved	-.31	-.18	-.22
Heavily involved	.27	.32	.39

a. All the significant discriminant functions have *p* < .01.

occurs: the heavily involved group perceives teaching and the preparation of school educators as more supported than the other three groups; the heavily involved group also holds that teaching and the preparation of school educators have and should have more weight for tenure consideration than the other three groups.

In addition to the consistent differences between the heavily involved group and the other groups, a general picture is depicted regarding the education faculty's perception of support and tenure consideration in relation to missions of the school of education. The group heavily involved in the preparation of teachers perceives that teaching and education of school educators are and should be supported by the school of education. The not so involved groups hold just the opposite perception. The discriminant analyses suggest that the faculty fragmentation is institutionalized in schools of education.

Research and the Preparation of School Teachers in the Tenure Equation

The survey respondents were asked to report their perceptions of the weight placed by their institutions on research and the preparation of school teachers for tenure consideration. They were also asked how the weight should be placed on research and the preparation of teachers for tenure purposes. The responses are reported in Table 7.3.

Table 7.3

Perceived and Desirable Weights of the Preparation of School Teachers and Research in Tenure Decision-Making[a]

| Group | Perceived Weight | | Desirable Weight | |
	Preparation of teachers	Research	Preparation of teachers	Research
Not at all involved	2.42	3.59	2.99	3.38
Marginally involved	2.27	3.60	2.97	3.36
Moderately involved	2.53	3.55	3.19	3.30
Heavily involved	2.85	3.58	3.58	3.20

a. The figures are means on a 4-point scale with increasing importance.

Some observations can be drawn from Table 7.3. First, where the education faculty's perceived tenure criterion is concerned, all four groups respond that research has more weight than the preparation of school teachers. This discrepancy in the perceived importance of research and the preparation of school teachers reflects, to a great degree, the reality of the reward structure in the school of education. Secondly, all four groups hold that the preparation of teachers should deserve a higher weight in the tenure equation. However, the difference between perceived and desirable weights is different for each group, with the not-at-all involved group having a difference of .57 and the heavily involved group a difference of .73. Faculty members who are heavily involved in the preparation of school teachers have a more intense desire to raise the weight of the preparation of teachers in the tenure formula. Thirdly, as illustrated in the second point, all four groups hold that research should have a less prominent role in making tenure-related decisions. Finally, it is interesting to note that where desirable weights of research and the preparation of school teachers are concerned, research still has a higher weight than the preparation of school teachers in all the groups except for the heavily involved group, which holds that the preparation of teachers should have a higher weight than research.

The above contrasts reveal the tension between research and the preparation of school teachers in the reward structure. As is illustrated in the previous section, when the education faculty is taken as a whole, there is a negative correlation between current involvement in research and in the preparation of school teachers. Where desirable weights are concerned, three out of four groups (except for the heavily involved group) still hold that research should have a higher weight than the preparation of teachers. The data indicate that the education faculty predict and expect that their engagement in research is required in order to obtain tenure.

What Will the Future Hold?

Different groups of the education faculty show both similarities and differences in terms of whether they think the importance of teaching, research, preparation of school teachers, and other missions of the school of education will likely change over the next three to five years. They were asked to respond by using a 3-point scale, with 1 meaning "likely to decrease in importance," 2 meaning "likely to remain the same," and 3 meaning "likely to increase in importance." The results are summarized in Table 7.4.

The essential theme of Table 7.4 is that all four groups predict an increase in the importance of all missions of the school of education. Many observations could be drawn from Table 7.4, but this author would like to make three points in relation to the topic of this chapter. First, the group heavily involved in the preparation of school teachers predicts the greatest amount of increase of importance in almost all missions. In comparison to the not-at-all and marginally involved groups, there is greater pressure on the heavily involved group to work on many fronts. Second, the heavily and moderately involved groups predict a greater increase in importance of the preparation of school teachers than the not-at-all and marginally involved groups. The discrepancy between the faculty members who are involved and not so involved in teacher education is likely to continue and exacerbate, which will lead to further fragmentation. Finally, all four groups predict that the increase of the importance of research will be greater than that of the preparation of school teachers.

In relation to the faculty's prediction of the importance of various missions of the school of education, they were also asked to rate their future involvement in the missions on a 3-point scale (Table 7.5), with 1 meaning "likely to decrease in involvement," 2 meaning "likely to remain the same," and 3 meaning "likely to increase in involvement." The message from the respondents is consistent with their predictions. On the one hand, all groups, except for the "not-at-all involved" group, expect themselves to be more involved in the preparation of school teachers, with the heavily involved group having the greatest mean (2.34). On the other hand, all groups will involve themselves more in research and scholarly productivity, with the moderately and heavily involved groups having larger means (2.39 and 2.35, respectively). For each group, the increase in future engagement in research and scholarly productivity is greater than the increase in the preparation of school teachers, except for the "not-at-all involved" group, which indicates less involvement in the preparation of school teachers. The heavily involved group indicates great increases in future involvement in teaching, research, effecting changes in public schools, and the preparation of school teachers. There is tremendous pressure on this group to increase work output

Table 7.4

Predictions of the Importance of the Missions by Four Groups
with Different Levels of Involvement in the Preparation of Teachers[a]

Missions	Not-at-all	Marginal	Moderate	Heavy
Teaching	2.12	2.15	2.13	2.13
Research and scholarly activity	2.42	2.50	2.37	2.49
Development, dissemination, and demonstration	2.24	2.25	2.27	2.29
Ad hoc services to schools and other educational agencies	2.20	2.27	2.26	2.31
Effecting changes in public schools	2.28	2.33	2.39	2.39
Professional preparation of school teachers	2.18	2.25	2.25	2.30
Professional preparation of special educators	2.10	2.10	2.15	2.19
Professional preparation of school administrators	2.15	2.16	2.14	2.19
Preparation of researchers and/or university/college faculty	2.23	2.24	2.19	2.25

a. Figures are means on a 3-point scale.

Table 7.5

Future Involvement in the Missions by Four Groups
with Different Levels of Involvement in the Preparation of Teachers[a]

Missions	Not-at-all	Marginal	Moderate	Heavy
Teaching	2.08	2.05	2.15	2.26
Research and scholarly productivity	2.28	2.26	2.39	2.35
Development, dissemination, and demonstration	2.12	2.18	2.19	2.27
Ad hoc services to schools and other educational agencies	2.12	2.17	2.16	2.26
Effecting changes in public schools	2.13	2.18	2.30	2.39
Professional preparation of school teachers	1.86	2.08	2.15	2.34
Professional preparation of special educators	1.91	1.97	1.97	2.01
Professional preparation of school administrators	1.96	2.01	2.03	1.97
Preparation of researchers and/or university/college faculty	2.11	2.11	2.22	2.15

a. Figures are means on a 3-point scale.

on multiple fronts. The heavily involved group will continue to be involved in the preparation of school teachers, but they expect themselves to achieve in other missions of the school as well. There seems to be a diversification of professional focus for the heavily involved group, which attenuates their focus on the preparation of school teachers.

Teacher Education Reform: The Discrepancy Continues

The four groups with various involvement in the preparation of school teachers were asked to what extent (on a 7-point scale with increasing agreement) they agree or disagree that their teacher education programs currently need major structural changes. The means for the heavily involved group to the not-at-all involved group are 4.54, 4.68, 4.74, and 4.72, respectively. All four groups tend to agree that teacher education programs need major changes, which is in contrast to the previous finding that education faculty members are positive about their work and do not see the need to change (Ducharme & Kluender, 1990; Howey & Zimpher, 1990). Nonetheless, the not-at-all and marginally involved groups have greater means, which suggests that they perceive more need to reform teacher education programs than the moderately and heavily involved groups do. The not-at-all and marginally involved groups feel less satisfied with the current teacher education programs.

When the respondents were asked what their involvement would be if there was a reform, the responses are significantly different for various groups ($\chi^2 = 136.5$, $df = 3$, $p < .001$). Significantly higher percentages of the moderately and heavily involved groups (88% and 95%, respectively) want to be involved in teacher education reform than do those in the not-at-all and moderately involved groups (60% and 77%, respectively). Furthermore, the not-at-all and marginally involved groups have a significantly different perception of their responsibility to be involved in teacher education reform from the moderately and heavily involved groups ($\chi^2 = 174.1$, $df = 3$, $p < .001$). Only 58% of the not-at-all group perceives that it is their responsibility to be involved in teacher education reform, while the corresponding percentages are 89% for the moderately involved and 96% for the heavily involved group. There is a significant difference between the not-at-all and marginally involved groups and the moderately and heavily involved groups regarding their responsibility in reforming teacher education.

A Perspective from the Qualitative Interview Data

The interviews with faculty members also reveal that the current reward structure results in the fragmentation of faculty. Some faculty members feel that the reward structure is unified, but faculty members have different levels of support and resources. The faculty becomes fragmented because some are more favored than others in light of the reward structure. Some faculty discuss the fact that since research is a criterion—in many cases the only criterion—by which everyone is evaluated, there is a pecking order for faculty members:

> I know how to do research, mind you, got my doctorate in research and statistics, and I've a pretty fair reputation as a researcher, but now what we're doing is considered lesser quality, you know, like the only people who can do research are the people in the ed psych area and what we do is second-rate somehow. They don't tell you that directly, but that's the implication. We have unheard-of loads here. It's almost as if they are planning to get rid of us, because we have so much to do that we can't possibly do it all well, and then they'll have their justification to eliminate us. The pupil teacher ratio in two of the areas is 40–1, but in ed psych, it's 15–1. (Male, Professor of Science Education, in a major public university, 20 years)

> Research is valued very highly, of course, but some of us have an easier time of it than others. The foundations people aren't struggling with the problems we have, so they have much more time. The ed psych people have a service course or two, but that's all. We have to go after our own money, and we are doing it, we are getting the money. (Female, Professor of Special Education, in a major private university, 16 years)

The interview data also suggest that some senior faculty members are not willing to re-orient their work to the new reward structure. Thus, there is a division between those who are and are not following the current reward structure. As a result, the education faculty becomes fragmented:

Right now, we don't know what our mission is. There are lots of people who have been here 20–25 years. They were elementary school teachers before that. They haven't grown. They still think they are in public school. (Male, Professor of Secondary Education, in a regional public university, 14 years)

When I came here, it was teaching and community involvement. I got promoted that way. Now they want to make [research] an important item. Every time we get a new dean or vice president for academic affairs they make a big deal about research. Sometimes it seems they would like to have everything. I'll retire as an associate professor because I won't sacrifice my teaching for research. (Female, Associate Professor of Psychology, in a regional public university, 16 years)

[In speaking of a favorite project, one involving numerous professors over the years:] With the president's emphasis on research, a lot of faculty who had been glad to pitch in on [the project] all of a sudden found they didn't have the time, where's the payoff? they said. I guess I can't blame them. I'm a full professor. You can't teach an old dog new tricks, and like I said, I came here because I wanted to teach, and I was hired to teach and that's what I'm going to continue to do. (Male, Professor of Educational Foundations, in a regional public university, 20 years)

Summary and Policy Implications

The foregoing analyses indicate that the education faculty has become fragmented. Nearly 30% of the faculty members are either not at all or marginally involved in the preparation of school teachers, which used to be the sole mission for most of the schools of education. The group currently heavily involved in teacher education is significantly different from the other groups along the dimension of perceived and desirable importance of teaching and the education of school educators. This difference is likely to continue, which will lead to further fragmentation of the education faculty.

While the group not at all involved in the preparation of school teachers indicates their reduced involvement in teacher education in the future, the heavily involved group predicts an increase in the importance of all missions of the school of education and indicates higher levels of engagement in almost all the missions. However, it will be difficult, if not impossible, for the heavily involved group to excel in all missions of the school of education.

The rising importance of research by respondents is consistent with the finding that the scholarly productivity of education faculty is comparable to that of all college and university faculty (e.g., Burch, 1989; Ducharme & Agne, 1982; Wisniewski & Ducharme, 1989b). The foregoing comparison is largely based on quantity of publication. Pickett and Burrill (1994) argue that there is no significant difference between educational and medical research in study designs and approaches to analysis. Their study does not support the idea that educational research is somewhat less rigorous than the health sciences, although others (e.g., Clark, 1987; Schwebel, 1985, 1989) question the quality of educational research.

In light of present conditions and future trends, the following policy issues deserve our attention. First, given the fact that research is becoming more and more prominent in the reward structure, it is crucial to uphold the notion that teaching and service also merit reward (Boyer, 1990; Sirotnik, 1991; Wisniewski & Ducharme, 1989b). Second, there is also an equity issue in the reward structure. The "not-at-all involved" group seems to be rewarded on the sole basis of research and research-related activities, whereas the heavily involved group is expected to achieve in all the missions of the school of education. There is a misalignment between the work that the heavily involved group is doing and the reward structure with which their work is judged. The result of this inequitable reward structure is the marginalization of the heavily involved group and its primary job—teacher education.

The issue then becomes how to counterbalance the trend of marginalizing teacher education as one of the major missions of the school of education when the importance of research is rising. One of Goodlad's postulates suggests the solution: "Programs for the education of educators must enjoy parity with other campus programs as a legitimate college or university commitment and field of study and service, worthy of rewards for faculty geared to the nature of the field" (1990a, p. 55). However, as the reform efforts in the 25 sites of the National Network for Educational Renewal indicate (Goodlad, 1994b), making this postulate a reality is a tremendous task that schools of education face in the coming century.

CHAPTER EIGHT

The Future of the School of Education

This chapter discusses the implications of the findings. It was found in the previous chapters that research dominates the current promotion criteria, and that providing services to schools and, to a lesser degree, the education of educators, have low status in both faculty members' mission involvement and the current promotion criteria. These findings point to both the tension within schools of education and the tension between the conduct of, and the expectation of society for, the school of education. A discussion of the internal and external tensions forms the first section of the final chapter. It was also found in the previous chapters that there is some incongruence between mission involvement and promotion criteria. The current promotion criteria tend to be Procrustean and do not pay enough attention to faculty members' levels and patterns of mission involvement. In connection with these findings, the second section of this chapter inquires into a theorized typology of the relationship between mission involvement and promotion criteria so as to provide a framework for further discussion.

Internal and External Tensions

Internal Tension: Alienating Force at the Institutional Level

The discrepancy between the current promotion criteria and current mission involvement reveals the alienating nature of the promotion criteria, and the alienation is most obvious in the case of teaching and research. Across all groups of faculty members, teaching is consistently perceived as having the highest rank among all missions, with research occupying a position ranging from second for most faculty groups and fifth for faculty members in comprehensive universities. In current promotion criteria, however, research becomes the most rewarded mission as perceived by all groups of faculty members while teaching is the second most rewarded mission. The reversal of these ranks for teaching and research in current mission involvement and promotion criteria illustrates, to a certain degree, the alienating nature of the promotion criteria.

The mean difference between teaching and research in current mission involvement and current promotion criteria is more illustrative of the alienating nature of the promotion criteria. For instance, faculty members in research universities perceive that in current mission involvement teaching and research have means of 3.54 and 3.19, respectively, with teaching leading by a mean difference of 0.35; but in the current promotion criteria, teaching and research have means of 2.82 and 3.88, respectively, with research leading by a mean difference of 1.06. Therefore, from current mission involvement to current promotion criteria, the means for teaching decrease while those for research increase. The discrepancy between the teaching-oriented mission involvement and the research-oriented promotion criteria is one of the major aspects of the alienating nature of the promotion criteria.

Another aspect of the alienating nature of the promotion criteria is that education faculty members perceive that in comparison to their desired promotion criteria, the current promotion criteria are unified and Procrustean in two ways: first, the current promotion criteria, regardless of faculty members' mission involvement, assign relatively non-differentiated weights to the missions; and second, the current promotion criteria do not pay enough attention to individual faculty members' patterns of mission involvement. In short, the discrepancy between education faculty members' desire for more diversified promotion criteria and the current unified and Procrustean promotion criteria is another important aspect of this alienation phenomenon.

The alienating nature of the promotion criteria exposes an interesting and profound issue regarding the relationship between the individual and the organization. It is widely held that higher education institutions are more decentralized than most organizations (Baldridge, 1983), and therefore, faculty members should be able to stipulate a set of promotion criteria that is more compatible with their patterns of mission involvement. If this were the case, then the alienating nature of the promotion criteria would not exist.

Given the fact that individual faculty members are not satisfied with the current promotion criteria, and neither is the public, then why the school of education as an institution has a set of alienating promotion criteria, and how the promotion criteria have evolved into the present situation, become interesting questions. It appears that an organization is not simply the sum of individuals in the organization and that an organization has its own identity and may alienate itself from the individuals who make up the institution.

The foregoing discussion regarding organizations as an alienating force is developed from the perspective of the strain between the individual and the organization. To point out the alienating nature of the promotion criteria at the institutional level does not imply that no issues exist at the individual level. On the contrary, the low involvement in providing services to schools and effecting changes in public schools, and the relatively low weights of these missions in desired promotion criteria, should become a major concern. Therefore, there is a complicated relationship between individuals and the school of education in relation to mission involvement and promotion criteria. On the one hand, the current promotion criteria in the school of education are misaligned with faculty members' mission involvement. On the other hand, education faculty members' mission involvement and desired promotion criteria are not without issues. To ignore both issues will result in the perpetuation of the undesirable conduct of the school of education and its faculty, from the perspective of society.

External Tension: The Rise of Research and the Loss of Identity

The results of this study indicate again that research has dominated the promotion criteria. There is a well-developed structure that promotes the preeminence of research on campus. The promotion criteria, in particular, and perhaps the reward structure, in general, certainly are part of the structure. Given the stringent academic job market and the benefits associated with promotions, it could be imagined that the research-dominated promotion criteria have a powerful impact on faculty members and, particularly, on young faculty members.

Outside the institution, there are other factors fostering the development of the centrality of research on campus. In public opinion and in the media, research is always associated with the reputation of an institution and individual faculty members. Many of the ratings of higher education institutions are weighted heavily on how much grant money and how many citations are received by faculty members. Achievements in research would bring a faculty member professional recognition beyond the local campus, a reward that accomplishments in other missions such as teaching and service cannot bring. As Goodlad observed (1990b, p. 77): "For successful professors, research grants and accompanying scholarly production bring visibility, geographical mobility, and free trips (with honoraria) to faraway places. Fame as a teacher, on the other hand, rarely travels beyond the local campus."

There is a publishing industry that caters to, and capitalizes on, the "publish or perish" syndrome. According to the report of the National Enquiry into Scholarly Communication (1979, pp. 40, 84), in 1948 there were 35 presses that were members of the Association of American University Presses. Twenty years later, the number had risen to 69. The annual book title output increased even more rapidly, from 727 titles in 1948 to more than 2,300 in 1966, an increase of more than three-fold. Accompanying the increase of university presses is the proliferation of academic journals. For example, the number of journals in English and American literature rose from 39 to 114 from 1960 to 1975. Over the same period, journals in philosophy increased from 39 to 91. Therefore, there is an infrastructure both on and off campus to bolster the research-dominated promotion criteria. The momentum of this research-oriented promotion criteria cannot be underestimated.

The overemphasis on research transforms the individual's internal burning desire to conduct research to an external pressure, which is, as Smith (1990, p. 197) commented, a tragic consequence of the "publish or perish" phenomenon:

> Research is not a right and certainly should not be a requirement. It is only tolerable if it is the passionate pursuit of a problem or vision that obsesses the researcher and will not let him/her rest. It could be argued that all reasonable impediments should be placed in his/her path to test his/her resolve. Certainly nothing should be done to encourage research for the sake of research/publication.

Ironically, the research-oriented promotion criteria seem to promote the quantity rather than the quality of research. Under the pressure to publish, faculty members, and particularly young faculty members, tend to work on short-term projects and the so-called least-publishable units. Again, Smith (1990, p. 199) made the following observation on quality of research:

> the vast majority of what passes for research/publication in the major universities of America is mediocre, expensive, and unnecessary, does not push back the frontiers of knowledge in any appreciable degree, and serves only to get professors promotions.

Research-oriented promotion criteria fail to lead to high-quality research, but they lead to a loss of the identity of the school of education. Goodlad (1990b) commented that the academic box of time is finite: if more time is spent on research, some time must be taken from other missions. The analyses in previous chapters clearly indicate that the preparation of school educators no longer has a high weight in the promotion criteria. Nor is it high on the list of mission involvement. Schools of education no longer view the education of educators as their central mission. In other words, with the rising importance of research in both mission involvement and promotion criteria, the original identity of the school of education has been gradually lost.

The gradual loss of identity of the school of education undermines the legitimacy of its existence. It is difficult to imagine that the law school does not center on preparing lawyers, and the medical school does not focus on preparing doctors. Then what is the justification for the school of education not to treat the preparation of school educators as its central mission?

As a matter of fact, the dissatisfaction with the quality of elementary and secondary education and school teachers often leads to criticism of the education of educators, which in turn makes the school of education a target for criticism. There has been an argument for an alternative to university-based education of educators (e.g., Edelfelt, 1979; George, 1979; Nicklas, et al., 1982). Some states have enacted policies that enable the education of educators to take place in settings other than schools of education (Carlson, 1992; Watts, 1982; Zumwalt, 1991). A lack of centrality of the education of educators in the school of education threatens its very existence.

Since the mid-1980s, there has been a renewed interest in improving teacher education in the United States, which is manifested in such reports as the Holmes Group's *Tomorrow's Teachers* (1986) and *Tomorrow's Schools* (1990), Carnegie Forum's *A Nation Prepared: Teachers for the 21st Century* (1986), and Goodlad's *Teachers for Our Nation's Schools* (1990b), and also in reform initiatives associated with the National Network for Educational Renewal, the Holmes Group, and the Urban Network to Improve Teacher Education. There has also been some effort, such as the one under the auspices of the Danforth Foundation, to redesign the programs for preparing school administrators (Achilles, 1994). It seems that it is now a golden opportunity to change the orientation of the school of education and make it more devoted to the education of educators. If the current effort to revitalize the education of educators does not significantly achieve its goal, the legitimacy of the existence of the school of education will be under further attack.

The above argument for changing the current promotion criteria and reorienting the school of education is developed from the perspective of the self-interest of the school of education. The same argument could be developed from the moral ground. It is the moral responsibility of the school of education to be actively engaged in preparing school educators and to contribute to the betterment of education in lower schools. It is morally indefensible to lure or even coerce education faculty members into conducting mediocre research while not paying enough attention to the education of school educators. Although it is arguable that the school of education has a Janus-like nature (Clifford & Guthrie, 1988)—looking both to the educational practice in the lower schools and the inquiry ethos on campus—scholarly interests must grow out of and support the school of education's central mission of educating educators (Soder & Sirotnik, 1990). It is time to reclaim the lost identity of the school of education and reorient it to the education of educators.

Enhancing the Autonomy of the School of Education

The loss of identity of the school of education is largely due to the evolution of the institution in which the school of education situates itself and the subsequent overwhelming influence from other entities on campus. It is a common practice that the promotion recommendation will be sent from the school to central administration, which has the authority to make the final decision. Because the norm of arts and sciences is so prevailing, faculty members in the school of education are often judged by the criteria set for faculty members in the arts and sciences. The adoption of criteria for the arts and sciences faculty compels education faculty members to incline to the academic education rather than the professional education model.

In a personal communication with this author, John Goodlad commented that after leaving the University of California at Los Angeles, he realized that there seemed to be revised reward criteria for faculty members in schools of medicine and law, while the faculty members in education were judged by the criteria designed for the arts and sciences faculty. In other words, the reward structure of some professional schools has been somewhat more closely geared to their missions, but no such adjustment has occurred for the school of education. The report of the Review Committee for Education pointed out this issue a decade ago (Goodlad, 1984, p. 11):

> although designing a new and innovative school building would be deemed an appropriate element for promotion in schools of architecture and urban planning, an equally new and innovative program to go into it probably would not receive similar recognition in schools of education. Schools of education have been remiss—in part because of their longing for academic recognition—in not seeking significant inclusion of professional criteria in the guidelines

and processes of faculty appraisal. They might well have sought counsel from their counterparts in law and other professions.

As Clark (1989) observes, to improve academic status within the university context, schools of education follow norms from mainstream academe. Because the norms of arts and sciences are so prevailing, faculty members in schools of education are often judged by the criteria set for faculty members in other departments. The adoption of criteria from arts and sciences compels education faculty members to lean toward the academic education rather than the professional education model. It appears that the adoption of the norm of the arts and sciences is one of the culprits that leads to the misalignment between education faculty members' mission involvement and the reward structure. Schools of education must have the autonomy to develop reward systems consistent with their nature as professional schools.

The analyses in previous chapters find more similarities than dissimilarities in faculty mission involvement and promotion criteria across research, doctorate granting, and comprehensive universities. In Fairweather's (1993b) words, there seems to be a homogeneity of reward structure. Given the fact that doctorate and comprehensive universities are generally evolved from teacher preparation institutions, it is time to question whether it is constructive for doctorate granting universities and, particularly, comprehensive universities, to emulate research universities. The strength of schools of education and their universities perhaps lies in their diversity rather than their uniformity. Even for research universities, the question still arises as to whether it is appropriate to emphasize research to the extent that other missions are marginalized. To seek a balance between missions seems to be an issue facing all three types of institutions, and the meaning of "balance" should vary for different types of schools of education.

Although the discussion here focuses primarily on the school of education as an institution, much of the discussion might be equally applicable to other colleges and the university as a whole. The overemphasis on research indicates that higher education institutions are more interested in comparisons with their peers and are paying less attention to the public's voice (Smith, 1990). In essence, higher education institutions have been developing priorities in reference to their peers in the academic community. As Bok (1992) and Fairweather (1996) rightly point out, public trust is an issue that all units in higher education institutions are facing.

Two conditions must be in place so as to restore the identity of the school of education. First, schools of education must have the autonomy to develop their own reward systems so as to be consistent with their nature as professional schools. Second, the immediate environment of the school of education, i.e., the higher education institution itself, must also emphasize teaching and service so that a more conducive milieu would be created to encourage the school of education's reorientation to being a professional school. It is politically difficult, if not impossible, for a school of education to pursue a reorientation and reclaim its lost identity without reducing the "publish or perish" pressure campus-wide.

Toward an Understanding of the Promotion Criteria

A Typology of Promotion Criteria

Promotion criteria have two dimensions: items such as teaching and research by which faculty members are evaluated, and weights associated with the items. Both items and weights can appear in different forms and their combinations result in a typology of the promotion criteria.

An item may be an important evaluation criterion to all faculty members or to some faculty members. If an item is perceived to be an important criterion by all faculty members, this item becomes a component of the common core. In a particular institution, there are three possibilities regarding the items along which faculty members are evaluated: first, there is only the common core, which consists of one or several items; second, in addition to a common core, there are some other items that appear to be important evaluation items to some but not all faculty members; and third, there is no common core, i.e., every faculty member has a unique set of items along which a faculty member is evaluated.

The weight of each item can be homogeneous or heterogeneous. Homogeneity of weight denotes the unity of the weight for faculty members, while heterogeneity implies a variation of weight. As the analyses of high- and low-involvement groups suggest, for most of the missions, faculty members desire to have heterogeneous weights compatible with their levels of mission involvement. In comparison to the desired promotion criteria, the weights in the current promotion criteria are more homogeneous.

Table 8.1

A Typology of Promotion Criteria

item / weight	core	core plus other items	no core
homogeneous	type 1	type 2	type 3
heterogeneous	type 4	type 5	type 6

more individualized
———————————————————→

    The matrix of the evaluation item on one side and its weight on the other reveals possible forms that promotion criteria may take (Table 8.1). Along the item axis, from only a core to a core plus other items to no core, the promotion criteria become more individualized by taking individual faculty member's patterns of mission involvement into account. Along the weight axis, from homogeneous to heterogeneous, the promotion criteria also become more individualized by taking faculty members' levels of mission involvement into consideration. The matrix is designed to illustrate the major forms (as denoted by types 1 to 6) that promotion criteria may take. In reality, the forms are even more complicated than in the illustration. For example, the promotion criteria with a common core and other items might have homogeneous weight for the core, while having heterogeneous weights for the items other than the core.

    For simplicity of discussion, there are three major models of promotion criteria (Figure 8.1) as represented by type 1, type 6, and types 2 and 5. Type 1 represents the unified model for which core items are defined and the weight associated with each core item is also specified. Therefore, it is unified both in item and weight. If the unified model is in place, regardless of faculty members' mission involvement, each faculty member will be judged by the same set of items, and weights for these items are fixed and homogeneous. The unified model is bureaucratic and institution-oriented.

Figure 8.1

A Schematic Presentation of a Typology of Promotion Criteria

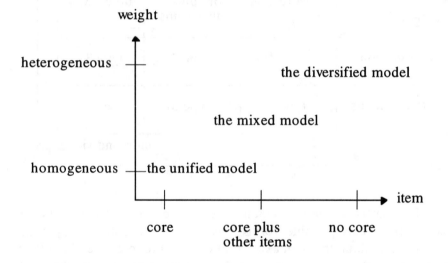

The diversified model, represented by type 6, does not define the evaluation items and the weights associated with these items. A faculty member may become involved in any legitimate mission, and a faculty member will be evaluated to a great extent by the activities in which this particular faculty member is involved. In contrast to the unified model, the second model is diversified in both item and weight, and the weight is in proportion to the degree of involvement. The diversified model, which is individual-oriented, takes into account the individual patterns of mission involvement. The drawback of the diversified model is that this model does not necessarily reflect an institutional identity, and it is extremely difficult to implement in practice.

Lying between the unified and diversified models is the mixed model. The mixed model defines a common core that is important to every faculty member. In addition to the common core, different faculty members are evaluated by their performance on other missions in which they are also involved. The weights for the common core and other items might be unified or diversified. If the common core and homogeneous weight represent the institutional dimension, other items and heterogeneous weights manifest the individual aspect. Therefore, the mixed model is a compromise between the individual and institutional dimensions. Along the directions of the arrows as illustrated in Table 8.1 and Figure 8.1, promotion criteria evolve from being institution-oriented to individual-oriented. The characteristics of the three models are summarized in Table 8.2.

Table 8.2

A Summary of Three Models of Promotion Criteria

	Model		
	The unified model	The mixed model	The diversified model
Orientation	institution-oriented	both institution- and individual-oriented	individual-oriented
Characteristic	procrustean items and weights for every faculty member	there is a common core and other items; weights for the core and other items might be unified or diversified	there is no common core and weights are diversified

The drawback of the unified model is the marginalization of those missions that are not evaluation items and those missions that become evaluation items but have low weights. For example, if effecting changes in public schools is not an item in the promotion criteria, or if effecting changes in public schools becomes an item in the promotion criteria but has a very low weight no matter how much a faculty member is devoted to it, there is simply not enough incentive for faculty members to be involved in effecting changes in public schools. In the context of the diversification of the mission of the school of education and its faculty body, the unified model faces a dilemma in stipulating items for the promotion criteria. On one hand, if the evaluation items only include one or two missions, other missions will be marginalized. On the other hand, if too many items are included in the promotion criteria, the items with low weights will be marginalized. In essence, the unified model, which expects education faculty members to have the same patterns of involvement in the missions, is incompatible with the diversified missions of the school of education.

In comparison to the unified model, the diversified model without core items and homogeneous weights goes to the other extreme. If the diversified model prevails in an institution, there seems to be no identity for this institution as reflected in the promotion criteria because, to a certain extent, the promotion criteria cater to faculty members' idiosyncrasies. As a result, there is no clear sense of institutional vision and mission.

The mixed model, which takes into account both institutional and individual dimensions, looks promising because it holds a common core for all education faculty members while giving them some leeway in terms of their involvement. This model is also more flexible in terms of the weights associated with each evaluation item.

As illustrated in Figure 8.1, the mixed model has a wide range. It seems that both the current and desired promotion criteria studied in previous chapters belong to the mixed model. However, the current promotion criteria differ from the desired promotion criteria on two aspects: first, the common core in the current promotion criteria is research, while it is teaching in the desired promotion criteria. Second, for most of the missions, the weights in the desired promotion criteria are more diversified than those in the current promotion criteria. Therefore, the current promotion criteria are more unified in comparison to the desired promotion criteria. This difference between the current and desired promotion criteria has policy implications for the faculty reward structure of the school of education, in general, and promotion criteria, in particular.

Policy Implications

On the basis of the empirical data, the explication of the typology of the promotion criteria, and the assumption that involvement in each legitimate mission of the school of education should be rewarded, the following policy recommendations are presented.

First, in a particular school of education, there should be a common core that is determined on the basis of institutional type, perceived visions and missions of the school of education, and other factors related to the locality. In essence, the common core represents the institution's identity. The analysis of high- and low-involvement groups' perceptions reveals that there is some tension between the current and desired promotion criteria, particularly in relation to whether research should be treated as part of the common core. The common core should be reached by discussion and consensus and should be conveyed in the same way to all faculty groups—male or female, tenured or untenured, and faculty members with different specializations.

Second, involvement in any legitimate mission of the school of education should deserve reward commensurate with the level of involvement. Generally speaking, the current promotion criteria have low weights for missions other than research and teaching. In other words, involvement in providing ad hoc services to schools and effecting changes in public schools will not be heavily rewarded regardless of some faculty members' heavy involvement in them. As was pointed out in the previous section, if some missions do not constitute the common core, faculty members who are heavily involved in these non-core missions should also be rewarded to the extent of their involvement. In other words, for the faculty who are heavily involved in non-core missions, these non-core missions should carry the maximum weight. Future promotion criteria should ensure that involvement in every legitimate mission of the school of education is rewarded to the extent of involvement. This recommendation moves beyond the prevailing recommendation in the current literature that we should reduce the role of research and increase the weight of teaching in faculty members' reward structure. This popular recommendation still neglects many other legitimate missions of the school of education and ignores the dynamics of the evaluation items and weights in promotion criteria.

Third, non-core items should have diversified weights for faculty with different levels of involvement. Weights for faculty members ranging from heavy to little involvement should also range from heavy to little weight. Diversified weights ensures that, in addition to the common core, faculty are promoted according to their achievement in the missions to which they have devoted most of their time and energy.

Fourth, the underlying idea of the aforementioned recommendations is that education faculty should be promoted according to their own patterns of mission involvement. Due to the diversity of missions of the school of education, individual faculty members' patterns of involvement in these missions are not the same. Therefore, the promotion criteria should also become more diversified and be consistent with individual faculty members' patterns of mission involvement. The analyses illustrate the urgency to make the promotion criteria more compatible with individual faculty members' patterns of mission involvement. However, the individual patterns of mission involvement should not be idiosyncratic, and it should contain the institutional aspect as reflected in the common core.

An Image of the Possible

Ideal promotion criteria have the following characteristics: a common core reached by consensus in a school of education; involvement in every legitimate mission of the school of education being rewarded to the extent of the level of involvement; items other than those that comprise the common core having diversified weights that are proportional to faculty members' level of involvement; and a catering to an individual faculty member's pattern of mission involvement.

The proposed promotion criteria belong to the mixed model and are similar to the desired promotion criteria as perceived by faculty members described in previous chapters. One caveat pertaining to the proposed promotion criteria is that it is not suggested that there is only one version of the proposed promotion criteria. On the contrary, there are many versions that depend on institutional context.

The proposed promotion criteria make compromises along the following aspects: individual inspiration versus institutional demand, core items versus non-core items, and homogeneous versus heterogeneous weights. The success of the promotion criteria depends on making contextualized balances between the extremes of these dimensions.

Coda

The school of education has lost its identity in the midst of its evolution. There is an internal tension between what education faculty members do and how they are rewarded. When the internal tension is viewed in a larger context, it becomes the external tension between the public's expectations for, and the conduct of, the school of education. These tensions have crucial implications for its health and well-being. The internal tension hurts education faculty members' morale, while the external tension influences the public's support for, and ultimately the legitimate existence of, the school of education. The school of education appears to be comfortable neither in academia nor in the public schooling sector.

The most serious challenge to the school of education is a trend toward educating educators in the school setting rather than in the university setting. This is partially due to the neglect of the education of educators in the university, and even in the school of education. It is time to reclaim its lost identity and make the education of educators the central mission. I would like to conclude the book with a quotation from the third report of the Holmes Group (1995, p. 17), *Tomorrow's Schools of Education*:

> Ambiguity surrounds the purpose of schools of education. Many of these institutions have been less than clear about their mission. The confusion arises, largely, from the tendency of many education schools to support too many different programs and to invest too little in work with the schools. As a consequence, a disproportionate number of faculty members separate their work from that of the elementary and secondary sector. Many professors go about their teaching and research with hardly a nod toward the public schools, seldom if ever deigning to cross the thresholds of those "lowly"

places. Such attitudes transmit an unmistakable message. The people most intimately responsible for children's learning in elementary and secondary schools are not sufficiently valued by the education school. Schoolteachers and young learners, who should be the focus of the education schools' concern, are kept at arm's length. They are a sideshow to the performance in the center ring, where professors carry out their work insulated from the messiness and hurly-burly of elementary and secondary education.

BIBLIOGRAPHY

AACTE. (1987). *Teaching teachers: Facts and figures.* Washington, DC: American Association of Colleges for Teacher Education.

AACTE. (1988). *RATE II. Teaching teachers: Facts and figures.* Washington, DC: American Association of Colleges for Teacher Education.

AACTE. (1990). *RATE III. Teaching teachers: Facts and figures.* Washington, DC: American Association of Colleges for Teacher Education.

AACTE. (1992). *RATE V. Teaching teachers: Facts and figures.* Washington, DC: American Association of Colleges for Teacher Education.

Achilles, C. M. (1994). Searching for the golden fleece: The epic struggle continues. *Educational Administration Quarterly, 30*, 6–26.

Aleamoni, L. M. (1980). *Developing a comprehensive system to improve and reward instructional effectiveness.* Paper presented at the National Faculty Evaluation Project Workshop for Community Colleges, Gainesville, FL.

Allen, F. C. L. (1990). Indicators of academic excellence: Is there a link between merit and reward? *Australian Journal of Education, 34*(1), 87–98.

Allison, C. B. (1989). Early professors of education: Three case studies. In R. Wisniewski & E. R. Ducharme (Eds.), *The professors of teaching: An inquiry* (pp. 29–51). Albany, NY: State University of New York Press.

Andersen, W. A., Cooper, J. M., DaVault, M. W., Dickson, G. E., Johnson, C. E., & Weber, W. A. (1973). *Competency based teacher education.* Berkeley, CA: McCutchan.

Applbaum, R. L. (1993). Scholarship reconsidered: A reflection. *Journal of the Association for Communication Administration (JACA),* (3/4), 25–30.

Babbie, E. (1989). *The practice of social research.* Belmont, CA: Wadsworth.

Bagley, A. (Ed.). (1975). *The professors of education: An assessment of conditions.* Minneapolis: Society of Professors of Education, College of Education, University of Minnesota.

Baldridge, J. V. (1983). Organizational characteristics of colleges and universities. In J. V. Baldridge & T. Deal (Ed.), *The dynamics of organizational change in education* (pp. 38–59). Berkeley, CA: McCutchen.

Beck, R. H. (1980). *Beyond pedagogy: A history of the University of Minnesota College of Education.* St. Paul, MN: North Central Publishing Company.

Bestor, A. (1985). *Educational wastelands: The retreat from learning in our public schools* (2nd ed.). Urbana and Chicago: University of Illinois Press.

Bok, D. (1991). The improvement of teaching. *Teachers College Record, 93* (2), 236–251.

Bok, D. (1992). Reclaiming the public trust. *Change, 24,* 12–19.

Borg, W. R. (1972). The minicourse as a vehicle for changing teaching behavior. *Journal of Educational Psychology, 63,* 572–579.

Borrowman, M. L. (1956). *The liberal and technical in teacher education: A historical survey of American thought.* New York: Bureau of Publications, Teachers College, Columbia University.

Borrowman, M. L. (1965). Liberal education and the professional preparation of teachers. In M. L. Borrowman (Ed.), *Teacher education in America: A documentary history* (pp. 1–53). New York: Teachers College Press.

Borrowman, M. L. (1975). About professors of education. In A. Bagley (Ed.), *The professors of education: An assessment of conditions* (pp. 55–60). Minneapolis: Society of Professors of Education, College of Education, University of Minnesota.

Boyer, E. L. (1986). Foreword. In B. R. Clark, *The academic life: Small worlds, different worlds*. Princeton, NJ: The Carnegie Foundation for the Advancement of Teaching.

Boyer, E. L. (1987). *College: The undergraduate experience in America*. New York: Harper and Row.

Boyer, E. L. (1990). *Scholarship reconsidered: Priorities of the professoriate*. Princeton, NJ: The Carnegie Foundation for the Advancement of Teaching.

Boyes, W. T., Happel, S. K., & Hogan, T. D. (1984). Publish or perish: Fact or fiction. *Journal of Economic Education, 15*(2), 136–141.

Brickman, W. W. (1986). *Pedagogy, professionalism, and policy: History of the Graduate School of Education at the University of Pennsylvania*. Philadelphia: University of Pennsylvania.

Burch, B. G. (1989). Perceptions of the role and scholarly reputation of the education professoriate. In R. Wisniewski & E. R. Ducharme (Eds.), *The professors of teaching: An inquiry* (pp. 87–104). Albany, NY: State University of New York Press.

Carlson, K. (1992). New Jersey's Alternate Route. In H. D. Gideonse (Ed.), *Teacher education policy: Narratives, stories, and cases* (pp. 73–90). Albany, NY: State University of New York Press.

Carnegie Forum on Education and the Economy. (1986). *A nation prepared: Teachers for the 21st century*. Washington, DC: Author.

Carnegie Foundation for the Advancement of Teaching. (1987). *A classification of institutions of higher education*. Princeton, NJ: Author.

Carnegie Foundation for the Advancement of Teaching. (1989). *The condition of the professoriate: Attitudes and trends, 1989*. Princeton, NJ: Author.

Cartter, A. (1977). The Cartter report on the leading schools of education, law, and business. *Change, 9*, 44–48.

Charters, W. W., & Waples, D. (1929). *The commonwealth teacher-training study*. Chicago: The University of Chicago Press.

Clark, B. R. (1987). *The academic life: Small worlds, different worlds*. Princeton, NJ: The Carnegie Foundation for the Advancement of Teaching.

Clark, B. R. (1989). Schools of education: The academic-professional seesaw. *Change, 21* (1), 60–62.

Clifford, G. J., & Guthrie, J. W. (1988). *Ed school*. Chicago: University of Chicago Press.

Cohen, A. M., Birnbaum, R., Pfnister, A. O., & Geiger, R. L. (1985). *Contexts for learning: The major sectors of American higher education*. Washington, DC: U.S. Government Printing Office.

Cohen, S. (1974). *Education in the United States: A documentary history* (Vols. 1–5). New York: Random House.

Compayre, G. (1885/1899). *The history of pedagogy* (W. H. Payne Trans.). Boston: D. C. Heath & Company.

Cremin, L. A. (1980). *American education: The national experience 1783–1876*. New York: Harper & Row.

Culbertson, J. A. (1988). A century's quest for a knowledge base. In N. J. Boyan (Ed.), *Handbook of research on educational administration* (pp. 3–26). New York: Longman.

Darling-Hammond, L. (1994). Developing professional development schools: Early lessons, challenges, and promise. In L. Darling-Hammond (Ed.), *Professional development schools: Schools for developing a profession* (pp. 1–27). New York: Teachers College Press.

Dewey, J. (1896). *Letter to the Board of Trustees of the University of Chicago*.

Dewey, J. (1904). The relation of theory to practice in education. In C. A. McMurry (Ed.), *The relation of theory to practice in the education of teachers* (pp. 9–30), The third yearbook of the National Society for the Scientific Study of Education, part 1. Chicago: University of Chicago.

Dewey, J. (1929). *The sources of a science of education*. New York: Horace Liveright.

Dill, D. D., & Associates (1990). *What teachers need to know*. San Francisco: Jossey-Bass.

Dixon, P. N., & Ishler, R. E. (1992). Professional development schools: Stages in collaboration. *Journal of Teacher Education, 43*, 28–34.

Ducharme, E. R. (1987). Professors of education: Beasts of burden, facilitators, or academicians. *Journal of Human Behavior and Learning, 4*, 1–9.

Ducharme, E. R. (1993). *The lives of teacher educators*. New York: Teachers College, Columbia University.

Ducharme, E. R., & Agne, R. M. (1982). The education professoriate: A research-based perspective. *Journal of Teacher Education, 33* (6), 30–36.

Ducharme, E. R., & Agne, R. M. (1986). Professors of education: Uneasy residents of academe. In R. Wisniewski & E. Ducharme (Eds.), *The professors of teaching: An inquiry* (pp. 67–86). Albany: State University of New York Press.

Ducharme, E. R., & Kluender, M. M. (1990). The RATE study: The faculty. *Journal of Teacher Education, 41* (4), 45–49.

Dunkin, M. J., & Biddle, B. J. (1974). *The study of teaching.* New York: Holt, Rinehart and Winston.

Edelfelt, R. (1979). Rethinking the role and function of the school of education. In *Alternative images of the future: Scenarios for education and the preparation of teachers* (pp. 28–42). Cedar Falls, IA: University of Northern Iowa.

Eells, W. C. (1963). *Degrees in higher education.* Washington, DC: The Center for Applied Research in Education.

Fairweather, J. S. (1992). *Teaching and the faculty reward structure: Relationships between faculty activities and compensation.* Washington, DC: Office of Educational Research and Improvement.

Fairweather, J. S. (1993a). Academic values and faculty rewards. *The Review of Higher Education, 17* (1), 43–68.

Fairweather, J. S. (1993b). Faculty reward structures: Toward institutional and professional homogenization. *Research in Higher Education, 34* (5), 603–623.

Fairweather, J. S. (1993c). Faculty reward reconsidered: The nature of tradeoffs. *Change, 25* (4), 44–47.

Fairweather, J. S. (1996). *Faculty work and public trust.* Boston: Allyn and Bacon.

Feldman, K.A. (1987). Research productivity and scholarly accomplishment of college teachers as related to their instructional effectiveness: A review and exploration. *Research in Higher Education, 26* (3), 227–298.

Finkelstein, B. (1982). Technicians, mandarins, and witnesses: Searching for professional understanding. *Journal of Teacher Education, 33* (3), 25–27.

Flexner, A. (1930). *Universities: American, German, English.* New York: Oxford University Press.

Fulton, O., & Trow, M. (1974). Research activity in higher education. *Sociology of Education 47* (1), 29–73.

Gage, N. L. (1979). *The scientific basis of the art of teaching*. New York: Teachers College Press.

Gage, N. L. (1985). *Hard gains in the soft sciences: The case of pedagogy*. Bloomington, IN: Phi Delta Kappa.

George, P. (1979). Teacher education: 1984 and 2001. In *Alternative images of the future: Scenarios for education and the preparation of teachers* (pp. 54–68). Cedar Falls, IA: University of Northern Iowa.

Gideonse, H. (1989). The uses of time: Evocation of an ethos. In R. Wisniewski & E. Ducharme (Eds.), *The professors of teaching: An inquiry* (pp. 119–133). Albany: State University of New York Press.

Good, C. V. (Ed.). (1959). *Dictionary of education* (2nd ed.). New York: McGrawHill.

Goodlad, J. I. (1984). *A place called school*. New York: McGraw-Hill.

Goodlad, J. I. (1990a). Studying the education of educators: From conceptions to findings. *Phi Delta Kappan, 71* (9), 698–701.

Goodlad, J. I. (1990b). *Teachers for our nation's schools*. San Francisco: Jossey-Bass.

Goodlad, J. I. (1994a). *Educational renewal: Better teachers, better schools*. San Francisco: Jossey-Bass.

Goodlad, J. I. (1994b). The National Network for Educational Renewal. *Phi Delta Kappan, 75* (8), 632–638.

Goodlad, J. I. (1994c). *What schools are for* (2nd ed.). Bloomington: Phi Delta Kappa.

Goodlad, J. I., Soder, R., & Sirotnik, K. A. (Eds.). (1990). *The moral dimensions of teaching*. San Francisco: Jossey-Bass.

Grossman, P. L. (1990). *The making of a teacher: Teacher knowledge and teacher education*. New York: Teachers College Press.

Grossman, P. L. (1994). *Preparing teachers of substance: Prospects for joint work, occasional paper No. 20*. Seattle: Center for Educational Renewal, College of Education, University of Washington.

Hailman, W. N. (1874). *History of pedagogy*. New York: American Book Company.

Harper, C. A. (1935). *Development of the teachers college in the United States*. Bloomington, IL: McKnight & McKnight.

Hazlett, J. (1989). Education professors: The centennial of an identity crisis. In R. Wisniewski & E. Ducharme (Eds.), *The professors of teaching: An inquiry* (pp. 110–128). Albany, NY: State University of New York Press.

Henderson, E. N. (1913). Pedagogy. In P. Monroe (Ed.), *A cyclopedia of education* (Vol. 4) (pp. 621–622). New York: Macmillan.

Herbst, J. (1987). *And sadly teach: Teacher education and professionalization in American culture.* Madison, WI: The University of Wisconsin Press.

Hewett, E. C. (1884). *A treatise on pedagogy for young teachers.* New York: American Book Company.

Higgins, J. (1923). *Fundamentals of pedagogy.* New York: American Book Company.

Hirst, P. (1966). Educational theory. In J. W. Tibble (Ed.), *The study of education* (pp. 29–58). London: Routledge and Kegan Paul.

Hollis, A. P. (1898). *The contribution of the Oswego Normal School to educational progress in the United States.* Boston: D. C. Heath.

Holmes Group. (1986). *Tomorrow's teachers: A report of the Holmes Group.* East Lansing, MI: Author.

Holmes Group. (1990). *Tomorrow's schools: Principles for the design of professional development schools.* East Lansing, MI: Author.

Holmes Group. (1995). *Tomorrow's schools of education.* East Lansing, MI: Author.

Houston, W. R., & Howsam, R. B. (Eds.). (1972). *Competency-based teacher education: Progress, problems, and prospects.* Chicago: Science Research Associates.

Howey, K. A., & Zimpher, N. L. (1989). *Profiles of preservice education: Inquiries into the nature of programs.* Albany: State University of New York Press.

Howey, K. A., & Zimpher, N. L. (1990). Professors and deans of education. In W. R. Houston, M. Haberman, & J. Sikula (Eds.), *Handbook of research on teacher education* (pp. 349–370). New York: Macmillan.

Hutchins, R. M. (1940). *The higher learning in America.* New Haven: Yale University Press.

Jackson, P. W. (1975). Divided we stand: Observations on the internal organization of the education professoriate. In A. Bagley (Ed.),

The professors of education: An assessment of conditions (pp. 61–70). Minneapolis: Society of Professors of Education, College of Education, University of Minnesota.

Johanningmeier, E. V., & Johnson, H. C., Jr. (1975). The education professoriate: A historical consideration of its work and growth. In A. Bagley (Ed.), *The professors of education: An assessment of conditions* (pp. 1–18). Minneapolis: Society of Professors of Education, College of Education, University of Minnesota.

Judge, H. (1982). *American graduate schools of education: A view from abroad.* New York: Ford Foundation.

Kachigan, S. K. (1991). *Multivariate statistical analysis: A conceptual introduction* (2nd ed.). New York: Radius Press.

Kant, I. (1798/1979). *The conflict of the faculties.* (M. J. Gregor Trans.). New York: Abaris.

Katz, D. A. (1973). Faculty salaries, promotion, and productivity at a large university. *American Economic Review, 63,* 469–477.

Katz, M. B. (1966). From theory to survey in graduate schools of education. *Journal of Higher Education, 36,* 325–334.

Kerr, C. (1994). *Higher education cannot escape history: Issues for the twenty-first century.* Albany: State University of New York Press.

Kerr, D. H. (1983). Teaching competency and teacher education in the United States. *Teachers College Record, 81* (3), 525–552.

Kerr, D. H. (1987). Authority and responsibility in public schools. In J. I. Goodlad (Ed.), *The ecology of school renewal* (pp. 20–40). Chicago: National Society for the Study of Education.

Kiddle, H., & Schem, A. J. (1881). *The dictionary of education and instruction.* New York: E. Steiger.

Kramer, R. (1991). *Ed school follies: The miseducation of America's teachers.* New York: The Free Press.

Labaree, D. F., & Pallas, A. M. (1996a). Dire straits: The narrow vision of the Holmes Group. *Educational Researcher, 25* (4), 25–28

Labaree, D. F., & Pallas, A. M. (1996b). The Holmes Group's mystifying response. *Educational Researcher, 25* (4), 31–32, 47

Lagemann, E. C. (1997). Contested terrain: A history of education research in the United States, 1890–1990. *Educational Researcher, 26* (9), 5–17.

Lanier, J. E., & Little, J. W. (1986). Research on teacher education. In M. C. Wittrock (Ed.), *Handbook of research on teaching* (pp. 527–569) (3rd ed.). New York: Macmillan.

Lasley, T. (1986). Editorial. *Journal of Teacher Education, 37*(3), inside cover.

Lawson, H. A. (1990). Constraints on the professional service of education faculty. *Journal of Teacher Education, 41* (4), 57–70.

Lay, W. A. (1907/1936). *Experimental pedagogy* (A. Weil & E. K. Schwartz, Trans.). New York: Prentice-Hall.

Long, J. S., Allison, P. D., & McGinnis, R. (1993). Rank advancement in academic careers: Sex differences and the effects of productivity. *American Sociological Review, 58* (5), 703–722.

Lonsdale, A. (1993). Changes in incentives, rewards and sanctions. *Higher Education Management, 5* (2), 223–236.

Mancing, H. (1991). Teaching, research, service: The concept of faculty workload. *ADFL Bulletin, 22* (3), 44–50.

Maynard, J. A. (1924). *A survey of Hebrew education*. Milwaukee, WI: Morehouse.

McConnell, T. R., Anderson, G. L., & Hunter, P. (1962). The university and professional education. In N. B. Henry (Ed.), *Education for the professions* (pp. 254–278). Chicago: University of Chicago Press.

McLean, J. E. (1987). *A useful university departmental evaluation system*. Paper presented at the Annual Meeting of the American Evaluation Association, Boston, MA.

Mohr, B. (Ed.). (1990). *Higher education in the European community: Student handbook* (6th ed.). London: Kogan Page.

Moses, I. (1986). Promotion of academic staff: Reward and incentive. *Higher Education, 15* (1/2), 135–149.

Moses, I. (1987). Educational development units: A cross-cultural perspective. *Higher Education 16* (4), 449–479.

National Enquiry into Scholarly Communication. (1979). *Scholarly communication: The report of the national enquiry*. Baltimore: Johns Hopkins University Press.

National Institute of Education. (1985). *Contexts for learning: The major sectors of American higher education*. Washington, DC: U.S. Government Printing Office.

Neumann, Y., & Finaly-Neumann, E. (1990). The reward-support framework and faculty commitment to their university. *Research in Higher Education, 31*(1), 75–97.

Nicklas, W. L. et al. (1982). Field-based teacher education: Programs that work. *Teacher Educator, 18* (1), 2–9.

Pangburn, J. M. (1932). *The evolution of the American teachers college.* New York: Bureau of Publications, Teachers College, Columbia University.

Payne, W. H. (1887). *Contributions to the science of education.* New York: Harper and Brothers.

Pickett, W., & Burrill, D. F. (1994). The use of quantitative evidence in research : A comparative study of two literatures. *Educational Researcher, 23 (*6), 18–21.

Powell, A. (1980*). The uncertain profession: Harvard and the search for educational authority.* Cambridge, MA: Harvard University Press.

Powell, A. G. (1976). University schools of education in the twentieth century. *Peabody Journal of Education, 54* (1), 3–20.

Powell, A. G., & Sizer, T. R. (1969). Changing conceptions of the professor of education. In J. S. Counelis (Ed.), *To be a phoenix: The education professoriate* (pp. 61–76). Bloomington, IN: Phi Delta Kappa.

Pratte, R., & Rury, J. L. (1991). Teachers, professionalism, and craft. *Teachers College Record, 93* (1), 59–72.

Roberts, J. R. (1968). The quest for a science of education in the nineteenth century. *History of Education Quarterly, 8* (4), 431–446.

Roemer, R. E., & Martinello, M. L. (1982). Divisions in the education professoriate and the future of professional education. *Educational Studies, 13* (2), 203–223.

Rosner, B. (1972). *The power of competency-based teacher education.* Boston: Allyn and Bacon.

Rossman, J. E. (1976) Teaching, publication, and rewards at a liberal arts college. *Improving College and University Teaching 24* (4), 238–240.

Royce, J. (1891/1965). Is there a science of education? In E. L. Borrowman (Ed.), *Teacher education in America: A documentary history* (pp. 100–127). New York: Teachers College Press.

Rudolph, F. (1977*)*. *Curriculum: A history of the American undergraduate course of study since 1636*. San Francisco: Jossey-Bass.

Russell, S., Cox, R., Williamson, C., Boismier, J., Javitz, H., Fairweather, J., & Zimbler, L. (1990). *Faculty in higher education institutions, 1988*. Washington, DC: U.S. Department of Education.

Ryan, K. (1987). The moral education of teachers. In Ryan, K., & McLean, G. (Eds.). *Character development in the schools and beyond*. New York: Praeger.

Sarason, S. B. (1978–1979). Again, the preparation of teachers: Competency and job satisfaction. *Interchange, 10* (1), 1–11.

Schwebel, M. (1985). Research productivity of education faculty: A comparative study. *Journal of Teacher Education, 36*(4), 2–7.

Schwebel, M. (1989). The new priorities and the education faculty. In R. Wisniewski & E. Ducharme (Eds.), *The professors of teaching: An inquiry* (pp. 52–66). Albany: State University of New York Press.

Shen, J. (1995). Faculty fragmentation and teacher education in schools, colleges, and departments of education. *Journal of Teacher Education, 46* (2), 141–149.

Shulman, L. S. (1986). Paradigms and research programs in the study of teaching: A contemporary perspective. In Wittrock, M. C. (Ed.), *Handbook of research on teaching* (3rd ed.) (pp. 1–36). New York: Macmillan.

Shulman, L. S. (1987). Knowledge and teaching: Foundations of the new reform. *Harvard Educational Review, 57* (1),1–22.

Siegfried, J. J., & White, K. J. (1973). Teaching and publishing as determinants of academic salaries. *Journal of Economic Education, 4* (2), 90–98,

Simon, B. (1981/1985). Why no pedagogy in England? In *Does education matter?* (pp. 77–105). London: Lawrence and Wishart.

Simon, B. (1983/1994). The study of education as a university subject in Britain. In *The state and educational change: Essays in the history of education and pedagogy* (pp. 127–146). London: Lawrence and Wishart.

Sirotnik, K. A. (1989). *Studying the education of educators, technical report No. 2.* Seattle: Center for Educational Renewal, College of Education, University of Washington.

Sirotnik, K. A. (1990). On the eroding foundations of teacher education. *Phi Delta Kappan, 71,* 710–716.

Sirotnik, K. A. (1991). Making school-university partnerships work. *Metropolitan Universities, 2,* 15–24.

Sirotnik, K. A., & Goodlad, J. I. (1988). *School-university partnerships in action: Concepts, cases, and concerns.* New York: Teachers College Press.

Smart, J. C., & McLaughlin, G. W. (1978). Reward structures of academic disciplines. *Research in Higher Education, 8*(1), 39–55.

Smith, B. 0. (1980). *A design for a school of pedagogy.* Washington, DC: U.S. Government Printing Office.

Smith, P. (1990). *Killing the spirit: Higher education in America.* New York: Viking.

Soder, R. (1989a). *Faculty work in the institutional context, technical report No. 3.* Seattle: Center for Educational Renewal, College of Education, University of Washington.

Soder, R. (1989b). *Status matters: Observations on issues of status in schools, colleges, and departments of education, technical report No. 4.* Seattle: Center for Educational Renewal, College of Education, University of Washington.

Soder, R. (1989c). *Faculty views of schooling, schools, teaching, and preparing teachers, technical report No. 5.* Seattle: Center for Educational Renewal, College of Education, University of Washington.

Soder, R. (1990a). The rhetoric of teacher professionalization. In J. G. Goodlad, R. Soder, & K. A. Sirotnik (Eds.), *The moral dimensions of teaching* (pp. 35–86). San Francisco: Jossey-Bass.

Soder, R. (1990b). Viewing the now-distant past: How faculty members feel when the reward structure changes. *Phi Delta Kappan, 71* (9), 702–709.

Soder, R. (1991). The ethics of the rhetoric of teacher professionalization. *Teaching and Teacher Education, 7,* 295–302.

Soder, R., & Sirotnik, K.A. (1990). Beyond reinventing the past: The politics of teacher education. In J. I. Goodlad, R. Soder, & K. A.

Sirotnik (eds.), *Places where teachers are taught*. San Francisco: Jossey-Bass.

Soderberg, L. O. (1985). Dominance of research and publication: An unrelenting tyranny. *College Teaching, 33* (4), 168–172.

Spring, J. (1990). *The American school 1642–1990* (2nd ed.). New York: Longman.

Stevens, J. (1992). *Applied multivariate statistics for the social sciences* (2nd ed.). Hillsdale: NJ: Lawrence Erlbaum Associates.

Stoddart, T. (1993). The professional development schools: Building bridges between culture. *Educational Policy, 7*, 5–23.

Strike, K. A., & Haller, E. J., & Soltis, J. F. (1988). *The ethics of school administration*. New York: Teachers College Press.

Strike, K. A., & Soltis, J. F. (1985). *The ethics of teaching*. New York: Teachers College Press.

Study Group on the Conditions of Excellence in American Higher Education. (1984). *Involvement in learning: Realizing the potential of American higher education*. Washington, DC: U.S. Department of Education.

Su, Z. (1986). *Teacher education reform in the United States (1890–1986), occasional paper No. 3*. Seattle: Center for Educational Renewal, College of Education, University of Washington.

Tabachnick, B. G., & Fidell, L. S. (1989). *Using multivariate statistics*. New York: HarperCollins.

Tuckman, H. P. (1976). *Publication, teaching, and the academic reward structure*. Lexington, MA: Lexington Books.

Tuckman H. P., & Hagemann, R. P. (1976). An analysis of the reward structure in two disciplines. *Journal of Higher Education, 47* (4), 447–464.

Tuckman, H. P., & Leahy, J. (1975). What is an article worth? *Journal of Political Economy, 83* (5), 951–967.

Tuckman, H. P., Gapinski, J. H., & Hageman, R. P. (1977). Faculty skills and the salary structure in academe: A market perspective. *American Economic Review, 67* (4), 692–702.

Urban, W. J. (1990). Historical studies of teacher education. In W. R. Houston (Ed.), *Handbook of research on teacher education* (pp. 59–71). New York: Macmillan.

Veysey, L. R. (1965). *The emergence of the American university*. Chicago: The University of Chicago Press.

Wang, M. C., Reynolds, M. C., & Walberg, H. J. (1987). (Eds.), *Handbook of special education: Research and practice* (Vol. 1). New York: Pergamen.

Watts, D. (1982). Can campus-based preservice teacher education survive? *Journal of Teacher Education, 31*, 50–53.

White, E. E. (1886). *The elements of pedagogy*. New York: American Book Company.

White, W. T. (1982). The decline of the classroom and the Chicago study of education. *American Journal of Education, 90* (2),144–174.

Winitzky, N., Stoddart, T., & O'Keefe, P. (1992). Great expectation: Emergent professional development schools. *Journal of Teachers Education, 43*, 3–18.

Wisniewski, R. (1989). The ideal professor of education. In R. Wisniewski & E. Ducharme (Eds.), *The professors of teaching: An inquiry* (pp. 134–146). Albany: State University of New York Press.

Wisniewski, R., & Ducharme, E. R. (1989a). Why study the education professoriate? In R. Wisniewski & E. R. Ducharme (Eds.), *The professors of teaching: An inquiry* (pp. 1–10). Albany, NY: State University of New York Press.

Wisniewski, R., & Ducharme, E. R. (1989b). Where we stand. In R. Wisniewski & E. R. Ducharme (Eds.), *The professors of teaching: An inquiry* (pp. 147–162). Albany, NY: State University of New York Press.

Wright, F. W. (1930). The evolution of the normal schools. *The Elementary School Journal, 30* (5), 63–320.

Zey-Ferrel, M., & Ervin, D. (1985). Achieving congruent actions and intentions: An empirical assessment of faculty work in a regional public university. *Research in Higher Education, 22*(4), 347–369.

Zumwalt, K. (1991). Alternative routes to teaching: Three alternative approaches. *Journal of Teacher Education, 42*(2), 83–92.

APPENDIX

A Description of the Sample and Data Source

The data reported in this book were gathered during the Study of the Education of Educators (SEE), a national study of 29 higher education institutions directed by John I. Goodlad. SEE had a purposive, representative sample, and the 29 institutions were representative in terms of institutional type (according to the Carnegie Foundation for the Advancement of Teaching, 1987), geographic and demographic diversity (according to Bureau of the Census), religious/nonreligious affiliation, the public/private dimension, and the programs of education of educators. For a detailed discussion of the methodology of SEE, please refer to Sirotnik (1989) and Goodlad (1990a).

The SEE faculty questionnaire was mailed to 2,042 education faculty members at the 29 institutions; 1,217 returned the questionnaire, yielding an overall return rate of 59.6%. The return rates for each type of institution were as follows: research universities 49.9% (417/836), doctorate granting universities 77.0% (352/457), comprehensive universities 57.4% (401/699), and liberal arts colleges 94.0% (47/50). Given the rule of thumb that "a response rate of at least 50 percent is *adequate* for analysis and reporting. A response rate of 60 percent is *good*. And a response rate of 70 percent is *very good"* (Babbie, 1989, p. 242), the data appeared to be satisfactory for analysis.

In this book, education faculty members were defined as tenure-line faculty associated with the school of education. Therefore, respondents not on a tenure-line are excluded in the book except for the data in chapter seven where all the respondents are included in the analysis. After excluding the respondents not on a tenure-line, valid cases for research universities, doctorate granting universities, comprehensive universities, and liberal arts colleges were 312, 290, 316, and 30 respectively. For one comprehensive university, none of the respondents was on a tenure-line; therefore, this particular institution was excluded from the analysis. In sum, the data source for this study included 948 tenure-line faculty in 24 institutions: 312 faculty members in 8 research universities, 290 faculty members in 6 doctorate granting universities, 316 faculty members in 10 comprehensive universities, and 30 faculty members in 4 liberal arts colleges. Since there were only 30 respondents from the four liberal arts colleges, this group of faculty members was excluded from the sample when multivariate analyses were conducted to compare faculty members across institution type.

The primary unit of analysis of the SEE was each of the 29 institutions, including its school of education, programs for preparation of educators, faculty members, and students. The focus of the current study was solely on the faculty. From the perspectives of professional rank and gender, the characteristics of the sample for this book were similar to those of other national studies on education faculty members, such as Ducharme's (1993) inquiry, the 1988 RATE study, and the data compiled by the United States Department of Education (Russell, Cox, Williamson, Boismier, Javitz, & Fairweather, 1990).

Of the 948 respondents, 65.5% were male and 34.5% were female; 93% were white, 5% were black, and 2% were Asian/Pacific Islanders, Hispanic, or native American. The respondents seemed to be normally distributed by five-year age ranges: 25–29, 0.3%; 30–34, 3.0%; 35–39, 10.5%; 40–44, 18.9%; 45–49, 19.0%; 50–54, 17.5%; 55–59, 17.8%; 60–64, 9.3%; and 65 or older, 3.7%. More than 80% of the respondents were over 40. As to professional rank, full professors made up 43% of the sample, associate professors 33%, assistant professors 20%, and others 4%.

ACKNOWLEDGMENT

I wish to thank John I. Goodlad and Kenneth A. Sirotnik for their advice and encouragement when I worked on this book. I am grateful to them for the support and mentoring over the years.

I want to thank the publishers for the permission to use some of the materials in the following sources: Grossman, P. L. (1990). *The making of a teacher: Teacher knowledge and teacher education.* New York: Teachers College Press (© by Teachers College, Columbia University); Shen, J. (1995). Faculty fragmentation and teacher education in schools, colleges, and departments of education. *Journal of Teacher Education, 46*, 141–149 (© by American Association of Colleges for Teacher Education); Shen, J. (1998). Unity and diversity of promotion criteria in U.S. schools, colleges, and departments of education. *International Review of Education, 44*, 21–45 (© by Kluwer Academic Publishers); Shen, J. (in press). A principal components analysis of latent structures of mission involvement and promotion criteria. *Educational Research Quarterly.* I also want to thank Roger Soder for the permission to use the qualitative data collected by him during the Study of Education of Educators.

I would like to thank my wife and son for their love and support and my mother for her role model. To them this book is dedicated.

INDEX